HOUSE

European Union Committee

39th Report of Session 2006–07

European Wine: A Better Deal for All

Final Report With Evidence

Ordered to be printed 23 October 2007 and published 30 October 2007

Published by the Authority of the House of Lords

London : The Stationery Office Limited
£11.00

HL Paper 184

The European Union Committee

The European Union Committee is appointed by the House of Lords "to consider European Union documents and other matters relating to the European Union". The Committee has seven Sub-Committees which are:

Economic and Financial Affairs, and International Trade (Sub-Committee A)
Internal Market (Sub-Committee B)
Foreign Affairs, Defence and Development Policy (Sub-Committee C)
Environment and Agriculture (Sub-Committee D)
Law and Institutions (Sub-Committee E)
Home Affairs (Sub-Committee F)
Social and Consumer Affairs (Sub-Committee G)

Our Membership

The Members of the European Union Committee are:

Lord Blackwell
Lord Bowness
Lord Brown of Eaton-under-Heywood
Baroness Cohen of Pimlico
Lord Freeman
Lord Geddes
Lord Grenfell (Chairman)
Lord Harrison
Lord Kerr of Kinlochard
Lord Maclennan of Rogart
Lord Marlesford
Lord Powell of Bayswater
Lord Roper
Lord Sewel
Baroness Symons of Vernham Dean
Baroness Thomas of Walliswood
Lord Tomlinson
Lord Wright of Richmond

The Members of Sub-Committee D (Environment and Agriculture) who participated in this inquiry are:

Lord Bach
Viscount Brookeborough
Lord Cameron of Dillington
Lord Greaves
Baroness Jones of Whitchurch
Baroness Miller of Chilthorne Domer
Lord Moynihan
Lord Palmer
Lord Plumb
Lord Sewel
Viscount Ullswater

Information about the Committee

The reports and evidence of the Committee are published by and available from The Stationery Office. For information freely available on the web, our homepage is:
http://www.parliament.uk/parliamentary_committees/lords_eu_select_committee.cfm
There you will find many of our publications, along with press notices, details of membership and forthcoming meetings, and other information about the ongoing work of the Committee and its Sub-Committees, each of which has its own homepage.

General Information

General information about the House of Lords and its Committees, including guidance to witnesses, details of current inquiries and forthcoming meetings is on the internet at
http://www.parliament.uk/about_lords/about_lords.cfm

Contacts for the European Union Committee

Contact details for individual Sub-Committees are given on the website.
General correspondence should be addressed to the Clerk of the European Union Committee, Committee Office, House of Lords, London, SW1A OPW
The telephone number for general enquiries is 020 7219 5791.
The Committee's email address is euclords@parliament.uk

CONTENTS

NOTE: References in the text of the report are as follows:
(Q) refers to a question in oral evidence
(p) refers to a page of written evidence

FOREWORD—what this report is about

In our interim report (HL Paper 141 published on 23 July 2007) we set out our emerging conclusions on the European Commission's proposals for reform of the EU wine sector. We indicated there that we would present our final report after the summer recess and that this would confirm or modify our preliminary conclusions and at the same time explore some of the underlying issues in the EU wine industry.

Since we reported in July, we have heard the views of HM Government on the adequacy of the Commission's proposals. The evidence given to us by the Minister, Lord Rooker, is published with this report. Having heard the Government's view, we are able to confirm the overall position which we adopted three months ago—namely, that we regard the Commission's proposals as constituting an important step in the direction of setting the EU wine industry onto a sounder basis. While this is our view of the reform package as a whole, we have serious reservations about two specific proposals within it—to extend the current ban on new plantings from 2010 until 2013 and to prohibit the use of sucrose in wine making. In Chapter One of this report we set out the Government's views and present our final conclusions on the Commission's Proposal.

In Chapter Two we turn our attention to what we see as the underlying weaknesses of the present system and the changes, not so much in regulation as in mind-set, which need to take place if the Commission's proposals are to bear fruit and set the EU wine industry on course for a successful future. We deal with attitudes to wine production, which appear to be too oriented towards the needs of producers and not enough towards those of consumers; with changes in public attitudes to wine, which we believe the EU wine industry has been slow to recognise; with the different structure and *modus operandi* of the New World wine industries which have enabled them to achieve an increasing share of the EU wine market; with attitudes to wine-making; and with the need for more vertical integration of the industry, from wine growing, through production, to marketing. It is clear to us that significant changes in all these areas are needed and that, unless such change takes place, the legislative reforms which the Commission has proposed will have only limited effect.

European Wine: A Better Deal for All

CHAPTER 1: THE GOVERNMENT'S VIEW OF THE COMMISSION'S PROPOSALS

The Story So Far

1. In our previous report on this subject[1] we examined specific proposals[2] which the European Commission had put forward for reform of the EU wine sector. The regulations governing this sector of the Common Agricultural Policy (CAP) are complex and we therefore included in our report a short layman's guide to their main features. This can be found in Chapter One of our previous report, but for ease of reference the text of that chapter is reproduced at Appendix 3.

2. Our report was made to the House less than three weeks after the Commission's proposals had been published. Though we had taken much expert evidence over the preceding five months on the state of the wine sector, including visits not only to Brussels but also the two important EU wine-producing regions, the time available, if we were to present a report to the House before the summer recess, did not allow for either a detailed examination of the Commission's proposals or the taking of evidence on them from HM Government. We decided therefore to present an interim report, recording our provisional conclusions based on a first reading of the proposals, and to follow this with a final report, confirming or amending those conclusions, when the House returned in October. That is the purpose of this chapter.

3. In our July report we concluded that the Commission's proposals, considered as a package, were worthy of support, though there were some elements of them to which we were opposed or about which we had reservations. The Commission's main proposals and the conclusions we reached on them may be summarised as follows:

   (a) That all subsidised wine distillation should cease—Strongly support

   (b) That 'National Envelopes' should be allocated to Member States from the Wine CMO Budget to enable them to fund a range of approved activities—Support[3]

   (c) That there should be a programme of subsidies to encourage the grubbing-up of uncompetitive vineyards—Support

   (d) That the current ban on new vineyard plantings should be extended from 2010 to 2013—Strongly oppose

---

1 HL Paper 144, Session 2006–07

2 COM(2007)372 Final

3 In principle and subject to the formulation of satisfactory rules governing the allocation and use of National Envelopes

(e) That subsidies for the use of grape must in wine enrichment should be abolished—Support

(f) That the use of sucrose in wine enrichment should be prohibited—Oppose

(g) That a proportion of Wine Sector funds should be transferred from Pillar I of the CAP to Pillar II in order to fund Rural Development measures in wine-producing regions—Support

(h) That the rules governing the classification of 'quality' wines and the labelling of 'table' wines should be reformed—Support[4]

(i) That EU wine-making practices should be aligned with those recommended by the OIV[5]—Support

(j) That farmland taken out of wine growing should qualify for the Single Farm Payment—Support

4. Shortly after publishing our report we were able to take evidence from The Lord Rooker, Minister of State for Sustainable Food and Farming at the Department for Environment, Food and Rural Affairs (Defra) and to hear from him the Government's views of the Commission's Legislative Proposal. A verbatim record of the evidence given by the Minister is published with this report.

The Government's Views

5. Lord Rooker described the Commission's proposals as "very positive". The Government had some areas of concern but "by and large", he said, "we think they are very bold and we want to give them maximum support for the issues that are really serious—i.e. that artificial market support should cease" (Q 906). The Minister warned, however, that getting agreement even to the Commission's reform package, let alone to the adjustments to it which the Government wished to see, would not be easy. "Some of the Member States do not want to move", he told us. "They are living in the past. They would like to carry on with all the market support, to have control over who can grub up and who cannot, to do things on labels that are still meaningless to consumers while allowing the competition from the New World to sweep the board" (Q 907). He instanced the desire of a few Member States to see the Commission's proposal to extend the ban on new plantings taken even further—from 2013 to 2015 or 2016 (QQ 907, 917). The Minister believed, however, that the Commission itself was in no doubt as to the need for reform and was doing its best to bring "old-fashioned conservative producers" into the 21st century (Q 922).

Distillation

6. Turning to specifics, Lord Rooker welcomed the Commission's proposal to end all subsidies for wine distillation. The present regime of subsidies, he said, had done nothing to curb wine surpluses. "They have just carried on producing. You cannot think of a less value-for-money arrangement". Continuing, he told us: "We wish to avoid subsidies by the back door. We must not give them a route that still encourages them to over-produce ...

---

4 But with reservations

5 *Organisation Internationale des Vins*

The immediate abolition of distillation is something that is a sticking point for us" (Q 908).

7. **We concur with the Government's view that the ending of subsidised distillation is a *sine qua non* of reform of the wine sector. While most of the other measures proposed by the Commission are to be welcomed, the ending of subsidies for distillation is crucial to the success of the reform package as a whole. Without it, none of the other measures will be able to deliver the efficiency gains which are necessary to set the industry on its feet again. We therefore confirm our strong support for this proposal.**

National Envelopes

8. "We support the concept of national envelopes", said Lord Rooker in evidence to us. On the question of how such envelopes might be allocated to Member States, the Minister said:

> "It is clear, on what figures we have seen, that France, Italy and Spain will be the recipients of most of the support … I think that is something we have got to live with because it is part of the price of stopping … the crude market support of distillation" (Q 911).

Robin Manning, Head of Cereals and Wine Division at Defra, added:

> "What we have said through the negotiation so far is that we can understand a lot of money going to the countries who have to make the biggest adaptations at the start of the transition period, but that, as you get into a steady state, it would make much more sense in many ways to start reducing the amount of money which is being spent on the wine regime" (Q 911).

9. We were particularly interested to have the Government's view on the overall scale of financial support for the wine sector. The Commission has taken the view that the reform process should be budget-neutral, over which we ourselves expressed some reservations in our earlier report[6]. Lord Rooker presented the Government's view of the matter as follows:

> "Yes, there should be savings but they are not going to be immediate. As part of the price … for getting what is a fairly large cultural change, as well as economic and management change, starting off with this new regime, as it were, budget-neutral is a way to try and win support … The budget is the maximum spend—there cannot be any increase on that. It would be nice if one could say there would be substantial cuts now, but that would probably negate the negotiating position of trying to get the change in" (Q 913).

10. **We confirm our acceptance of the concept of national envelopes. While an allocation formula for national envelopes which gives priority to the main wine-producing States is acceptable in the short term, the medium term aim should be to reduce wine sector funding overall and to re-assess the allocation of national envelopes among Member States.**

11. There remains the question of how national envelopes might appropriately be used. Robin Manning described the Government's objective this way:

---

6 See HL 144-I, Paragraphs 60–63

> "What we want to do most of all is to avoid measures coming into the national envelopes which try and perpetuate the lack of market focus that we see at the moment. So far as we are concerned, we can probably live with the measures which are in the national envelopes; we would not be keen about adding to them" (Q 911).

12. Against this background we asked what was the Government's view of the proposal to allow the use of national envelopes to fund 'Green Harvest'—i.e. the picking and disposal of unripe grapes where there is an excess of supply over demand. The Minister accepted that there was "quite a lot of scepticism" about the proposal to allow Member States to use national envelope funding for this purpose. He felt, however, that such schemes were "probably less damaging than the support systems we have at the moment" and that 'Green Harvest' would have a less distorting effect on the market than subsidised distillation. He felt therefore that the Government might be prepared to accept such a subsidy on the understanding that it would not form a permanent part of the Wine CMO and in the belief that few, if any, Member States would wish to devote national envelope funds to it because it would be difficult to administer and would be unlikely to have any significant market impact (Q 910).

13. More generally, Lord Rooker told us that "we want, frankly, as much of the money as we can get swapped over to Pillar II" (Q 911). Not only would this offer more appropriate avenues than exist at present for addressing the problems of the wine industry but it would also oblige Member States to co-finance. "They would have to pay more themselves", said the Minister, "There would be pressure on the Member States not to do silly things" (Q 912).

14. **We support the Government's view regarding the use of national envelopes—that they should be used for purposes which will promote the efficiency of the wine sector or address the consequences of its reform and that the most suitable way of achieving this is via transfer of funds from Pillar I to Pillar II of the CAP. For this reason we do not support the inclusion of 'Green Harvest' among eligible measures for funding from national envelopes and we confirm our opposition to this proposal.**

Grubbing-Up

15. We took no further evidence from the Government on this proposal. The Government had indicated general support for a grubbing-up programme in its evidence earlier this year[7] and we have no reason to believe that this position has changed.

16. **We confirm our support for a programme of voluntary grubbing-up of uncompetitive vineyards and we reiterate our wish to see tight definition of the exemptions which Member States may invoke to block grubbing-up applications by wine growers.**

The Ban on New Plantings

17. The Commission is proposing to extend the current ban on new vineyard plantings from 2010 to 2013. Lord Rooker questioned the logic of even the

---

7 See, for example, HL144-II, Q 31

existing ban. "It is very hard", he said, "to understand why the producer Member States attach so much significance to the planting rights scheme and consider it a success, when you consider the problems facing the wine sector at the moment" (Q 917). It is clear enough to us as a committee why there is such pressure to extend the current ban, even beyond the Commission's proposed deadline of 2013. The usual reason given is that it is inconsistent to liberalise new plantings at the same time as having a subsidised grubbing-up programme. We have already dealt with this objection in our previous report: if subsidised distillation is abolished, as is proposed, there will be no risk of new entrants to the wine industry planting vineyards for whose product they cannot foresee a clear market outlet. We cannot help feeling, however, that there is another reason why planting bans are so favoured in some quarters—namely, that they prevent entrepreneurial new wine-growers from entering the industry and presenting uncomfortable competition for existing uncompetitive growers.

18. The Minister clearly recognised this situation. He told us:

> "If someone is going to plant a vineyard, they ought to do it in the knowledge that they think they can sell and market their product. That is the point. There should not be a ban on plantings. They take the risk of planting; it should not be for individual producers to say: 'Ah, we are going to ban so-and-so planting extra, because that protects our little empire'. That is quite unacceptable" (Q 917).

And he added that:

> "we cannot possibly countenance a system of having bans on plantings, then trying to extend it and then individuals trying to decide who can plant what and where" (Q 917).

19. The Government's strategy, however, appears to be to acquiesce in the Commission's proposal to extend the current planting ban from 2010 to 2013 on two conditions—that under no circumstances will the ban be extended further and that in the meantime the threshold above which Member States come within the rules of the Wine CMO is raised from a five-year rolling production total of 25,000 hectolitres a year to at least 50,000 hectolitres (QQ 907, 930). The Government's prime concern here is to prevent artificial obstacles being placed in the path of the small but thriving UK wine industry, which is growing rapidly and is already close to the 25,000-hectolitre limit: once above that point, which is likely to happen within the next couple of years, it would be caught by the planting ban.

20. It would plainly be economic nonsense to impose an artificial planting ban on a Member State whose vineyards can sell all their produce and have no need of EU subsidies. Our own concern, however, goes rather wider. Planting bans are detrimental to efficient wine-growers across the industry as a whole. Much-needed restructuring cannot be expected to take place while uncompetitive producers are permitted to hide within the comfort zone of a regulation which bars enterprising new businesses from entering the market. We are reassured to hear that the Government shares our view. Whether the strategy of acquiescing in the ban to 2013 in return for other adjustments to the proposals is a wise one is another matter. Provided that the current Wine CMO threshold can be raised as the Government wishes, such acquiescence might be without cost to the British wine industry. But it would surely

postpone the day when the industry across the Community as a whole learns to confront inevitable market realities.

21. **We are pleased to see that the Government shares our view of the need to end the current planting ban. As regards the detail of this, we recognise that it is for the Government to make its own judgement of the situation, taking into account the concerns of the UK Wine Industry. However, it will be better for the EU Wine Industry as a whole if the ban is lifted sooner rather than later.**

Enrichment

22. Lord Rooker believed that the Commission's proposal to ban the use of sucrose for wine enrichment "would be very costly—an increase in production costs of 10–20 per cent" (Q 919). Robin Manning described the pressure for banning sucrose as "just a crude mechanism to try and use extra grape juice" and that it was recognised as such within the debate on wine sector reform. He added however that there was a great deal of opposition to the proposal and that "we do not think that the ban on sugar will last the negotiation" (Q 921). This confirmed the impression we had gained earlier in the year when taking evidence in Brussels from Member States. We are pleased to see that the Government shares our view of this measure, which would not only operate against the interests of wine producers in Northern and Central Europe but also put EU producers as a whole at a competitive disadvantage vis-à-vis their New World counterparts, where sucrose is widely used in wine enrichment. We hope that the assessment will prove correct that this proposal will not survive.

23. **We confirm our support for the ending of subsidies for the use of grape must in wine enrichment and our opposition to the proposed ban on the use of sucrose.**

Rural Development

24. In our earlier report we supported, subject to one caveat, the Commission's proposal to transfer a proportion of funds from the Wine CMO (Pillar I of the CAP) to Pillar II in order to fund Rural Development (RD) programmes, tailored to individual wine-producing regions, via national envelopes. The Government too was supportive of this initiative, partly because it was considered that RD programmes are a better way of addressing the social and economic consequences of reform than are market intervention measures and partly also because RD programmes are co-financed and Member States would therefore have an incentive to maximise value for money in funding them. We entirely concur with this thinking.

25. **We confirm our support for the transfer of a substantial proportion of Wine CMO funds from Pillar I to Pillar II of the CAP in order to support Rural Development programmes in wine-producing regions.**

26. However, as we remarked in our earlier report[8], one of the eligible RD measures in the Commission's proposals is the provision of what is called 'investment support' to wine producers who are obliged, as a result of the ban on the use of sucrose, to use grape must to enrich their wine. We drew

---

[8] HL 144, Paragraphs 30–31

attention to this issue in our first report and we asked the Minister for the Government's attitude to it.

27. The Government was inclined to take a somewhat more relaxed view of this proposal. Robin Manning said that "it would be for Member States to take a view on whether or not this is the sort of thing that they would want to invest in. But" he added, "given the small amount of money which is going into Rural Development ... I would think it would probably not be high on the list of priorities for any Member States" (Q 921). We are not wholly convinced by this argument. To some extent, there is a similarity here with the 'Green Harvest' issue[9]: if the proposal is regarded as acceptable on the grounds that few, if any, Member States are likely to take advantage of it, then we cannot help wondering what is the use of it. Moreover, what is being proposed here is that EU taxpayers' money be used, not in order to deal with a social, rural or environmental problem (the proper use of RD funding), but to counteract the effects of a proposed course of action (an obligation on wine producers to use expensive grape must for enrichment) which is unsupported by any rational argument and demonstrably inimical to the profitability of the industry as a whole.

28. **We re-state our opposition to the use of Rural Development funds to remedy an economic problem resulting from a proposed administrative measure (banning the use of sucrose in wine enrichment) which makes no sense in its own right.**

Wine Classification and Labelling

29. The Government shared our disappointment that the reforms in this area, useful as they are, preserved a situation which is essentially producer- rather than consumer-oriented. Lord Rooker felt that the maintenance of the link between wine quality and region of production failed to recognise that the mass consumer was "not part of the cognoscenti of wine drinking" and that he or she was not likely to respond to a system which required a degree of specialist knowledge of wine. "They have got to learn", said the Minister, "that this regime is not for the producer, it is for the consumer" (Q 922).

30. We endorse this view. The proposed new system of Protected Geographical Indications (PGIs) and Protected Designations of Origin (PDOs) is, of course, designed to bring the classification of wine into line with the arrangements which exist for other foodstuffs. But, as the names themselves imply, the emphasis appears to be on protecting the producers of such wines rather than on improving their marketing to consumer. The proposed removal of labelling restrictions on table wines will certainly help the marketing of such wines, and that is to be welcomed. Indeed, we would have wished to see the reforms in this area go further and permit all wine producers to describe their wines in whatever ways they wish subject only to the rule that what appears on the label must be honest and truthful. But maintenance of the link between quality and geography will do little to commend PGI and PDO wines to the mass consumer who has the alternative of buying good-tasting and easily recognisable brands from the New World. The new classification system has the appearance of a defensive withdrawal by the EU wine industry into a citadel at a time when it needs to be out in the field fighting for new customers.

---

9 See Paragraphs 12–14

31. There appears to us to be an overlap between the proposed new rules on wine classification and the proposal to extend the ban on new plantings until 2013. The Commission's proposal refers, under the heading of wine classification, to "expanding the role of the inter-professional organisations in order to be able to control and manage the quality of the wine produced in their territories"[10]. It also refers, under the heading of planting bans, to "Member States' competences regarding access to protected designation of origin or Geographical Indication status, for example area delineation, setting maximum yields and other stricter rules on production, processing and labelling"[11]. If this means simply that Member States and wine-making bodies will have a role to play in setting the parameters of PGI and PDO wines, fair and good. The wording, however, seems a little elastic and we are concerned lest the proposed 'competences' might be used, even after the end of the current planting ban, to prevent entrepreneurial wine makers from entering the market in specific regions.

32. There is a also a linkage between this issue and the proposal that in future some 10 per cent of the Wine CMO Budget should be devoted, via national envelopes, to promoting the sale of EU wines. In our report earlier this year we made a plea for promotion to be interpreted as marketing in its widest sense and, in particular, for money to be spent, less on advertising the perceived virtues of EU wines, and more on connecting the wine producer with the wine consumer, so that production is structured around what the market wants. It is clear from the evidence we have received in the course of our inquiry that one of the things that the mass consumer wants is wine which is presented to him in such a way that he can readily understand the product that he sees on the shelf—what it is made of, for what sort of occasions it might be suitable and what it is going to taste like. If the main selling point is going to be that the wine in the bottle comes from this or that chateau or vineyard, that is unlikely to make much impact or provide strong motivation for purchase among ordinary wine consumers.

33. **We confirm our earlier view that, while the proposed relaxations in labelling rules are to be welcomed, the proposed new wine classification system is unlikely to be sufficient to reverse the trend of mass consumption of non-EU wines. We also wish to sound a note of concern lest the new system could be used to prevent entrepreneurial new wine makers from entering the market after the ending of the current planting ban.**

Wine-Making Practices

34. We have taken no further evidence from the Government on this issue and **we confirm our earlier support for the Commission's proposal that OIV-recommended oenological techniques should become the benchmark for authorisation of wine-making practices within the EU.**

Single Farm Payment

35. In our earlier report we recorded our initial interpretation of the Commission's proposals in this area as being that all wine-growing areas should in future qualify for the Single Farm Payment (SFP) and that land

---

10 COM(2007)372 Final, Section 3.1

11 COM(2007)372 Final, Section 3.1

taken out of production under the proposed grubbing-up scheme should come within the ambit of the SFP[12]. Closer examination of the Commission's proposals, together with evidence from HM Government, leads us to believe that our initial interpretation was not entirely correct. Article 95 of the Commission's Legislative Proposal makes clear that wine growers who grub up all or part of their vineyards will indeed qualify for the SFP. But, Lord Rooker told us, "it is not giving Single Farm Payments for existing vineyards". Robin Manning added that "the only new entitlements which are being created by the wine reform occur where the farmer is actually undergoing a fundamental change in land use and, effectively, going out of wine production" (Q 925).

36. **While we consider there would be advantage in bringing all land producing food and drink, including vineyards, within the Single Farm Payment system, we nonetheless support the more modest reform of bringing grubbed-up vineyard land within the ambit of the SFP.**

37. Chapter Three contains a full list of our final conclusions on the Commission's Legislative Proposal. We make this report to the House for debate.

---

12 HL 144, Paragraph 27

CHAPTER 2: THE EU WINE INDUSTRY—SOME UNDERLYING PROBLEMS

38. In this chapter we look at some of the features of the EU wine industry which have come to our attention in the course of our inquiry and which seem to us to lie at the heart of the problem of over-production and declining market share. Our purpose in doing so is not to be critical of the EU wine sector so much as to highlight aspects of the industry which must change if the regulatory reforms proposed by the Commission are to have any chance of succeeding. Legislative reform is certainly necessary, but it is not the whole story: the mind-set which pervades much of the sector must change too.

Wine and the Consumer

39. The last 30 years have seen a noticeable change in attitudes to wine drinking. Until the 1970s wine tended to be regarded in Britain as either a product for connoisseurs (whether to collect or to drink) or a beverage to be enjoyed on special occasions, such as weddings, or—though the practice was not widespread—a drink to accompany meals. On the other hand, within many of the main wine-producing countries wine was regarded not only as a drink for connoisseurs but also as an everyday beverage for ordinary families at mealtimes. According to Philippe Casteja, former President of the Inter-Professional Council of Bordeaux Wine Makers (CIVB), the widespread consumption of non-high-quality wine derived historically from the variable quality of tap water in some Member States (Q 817)[13]. The result has been a dichotomy between wine for the specialist and wine for everyday use, which is to a large extent reflected in the current formal division of EU wines into quality and table wines.

40. Across Europe, as well as many other parts of the world, the situation today is very different. Dan Jago, Wine Buyer for the Tesco supermarket chain, put it this way:

> "We have seen an increasing switch of customers' use of wine from what was regarded as a slightly ethereal, heavy—if you like, snobbish—area of interest … to a much more mainstream product, and I think the fact is that wine is fundamentally an alcoholic beverage made from grapes that works extremely well with food, and customers are beginning to realise this" (Q 644).

Julian Dyer, Senior Wine Buyer for Sainsburys, agreed. "Wine is no longer just about special occasions", he told us, "it is about everyday consumption" (Q 654). Luigi Polizzi, Italian SCA[14] representative, said much the same thing: "Wine has become an occasion to drink in a group during the evening, so now the habits of young people have also changed" (Q 418).

41. This change has affected both the amount and type of wine being drunk. In Languedoc/Roussillon we were told by Bernard Clarimont, an official of the Regional Directorate of the French Ministry of Agriculture, that the market for table wines in France was falling by between 800,000 and a million hectolitres a year. "The people who consume these types of wine", he said,

---

13 References in this chapter are to the evidence published as HL 144, Part II

14 The Special Committee on Agriculture is an official level committee in Brussels which prepares the work of the Council of Agriculture Ministers

"are a relatively elderly population and this population is declining" (Q 747). In other words, the kind of ordinary *vin de table* which was once drunk with meals instead of water is in declining demand as a new generation comes along with new wine-drinking habits. Small wonder therefore that there are surpluses of such wines.

42. The character of wine being sought has also changed. There will always be a niche market for high-quality wines produced in particular locations or with specific characteristics. Mass consumer demand, however, is for something else. Today's mass consumer has more money to spend than before but he does not buy wine in order to lay it down as an investment or to enjoy it as an art form but rather to drink it with meals or on social occasions with family or friends. He is not interested in the cheapest wine but equally he has no wish to pay a high price for a wine whose incremental value is not apparent. Alain Vironneau, President of CIVB, told us in Bordeaux that "within the next five years your middle range of wines costing between $5 and $25 a bottle is going to account for 95 per cent of the wine market". He continued:

> "There are the Lamborghinis and the Rolls Royces, we have got them. But we have also got the Ford Pop, if I may stretch a point. 95 per cent is Ford Pop. There is a 95 per cent segment out there of people who want to drink Bordeaux wine, who would like to think that every time they open a bottle in the middle segment they are opening *Chateau Petrus* but of course they are not going to" (Q 816).

43. A crucial factor in all this has been the rise of the supermarket. Michael Paul, Chairman of the Consultancy *Wine Intelligence*, was clear about this when speaking of the situation in the UK: "If it had not been for the supermarkets embracing wine and making it a destination category, wine would not be in the position it is now, having grown at 5 per cent a year for the last 10 years" (Q 515). Julian Dyer told us that supermarket purchases accounted for some two thirds of all UK wine sales. Continuing, he said: "The growth in wine over this period has come about as a result of the supermarkets making wine more accessible ... easier to get hold of, easier to understand—and they have been merchandised in a way with which customers are familiar" (Q 651). The self-service character of supermarkets makes it easier for consumers to experiment with a commodity of which they know little and it has encouraged them to look for recognisable brand labels and special offers.

44. This process of demystification has been helped by the entry into the market of New World wines, which in many respects are produced and marketed in a different way from EU wines. New World wine producers have recognised that they are dealing with a new type of consumer, who is not—and does not want to become—a wine connoisseur but who wants to be able to acquire good-tasting wine at a reasonable price. They have therefore marketed their wines by using reference points, such as grape variety and brand name, which can be easily recognised rather than by following the European model of defining good wine by reference to a myriad of geographical indications. Luigi Polizzi, Italian SCA representative, agreed that this was a key area in which New World producers had scored. "The marketing is really well organised in these countries", he told us, "and they use easy communication with the consumer because they use four or five international varieties. In Italy we have different varieties in each region. It is really difficult to put that information in one line" (Q 382). Philippe Casteja agreed. He suggested to

us that French, Italian and Spanish wines were difficult for the new consumer to get to grips with and that they were "addressed to people who knew their way around wines". He continued:

> "We are facing, and have been facing over the last 25 years, new consumers. These new consumers did not have a clue what it was about and wanted something simple. They wanted a product that they could easily understand. That is why the answer has been—excuse me for thinking it is the French influence—that they have taken the Merlot, the Cabernet Sauvignon or Shiraz for the United States in order to use words which were known to make the offer easy ... The New World is an answer to new consumers ... The public nowadays is not a connoisseur type of public" (Q 810).

45. Where does this change in consumer habits leave the EU wine industry? In some difficulty, we would suggest. The problem seems to be that the industry has been slow to respond to the change—or in some cases even to recognise that it has taken place. There is undoubtedly a cultural factor at work here. Eva Corral, Head of the Wine Sector Division at COPA-COGECA[15], illustrated this when she referred to wine as "a product that is alive" (Q 234) and to the close linkage of wine production in the EU with locality or *terroir* (Q 242). Whatever the merits or demerits of this concept, it is but a short step from there to regarding wine production as more of a cultural craft in which the producer knows what is best than a straightforward commercial activity in which the customer is dominant. In Michael Paul's view, "the profit motive, which is what drives business fundamentally, does not exist in wine to the same extent that it exists in other categories" (Q 536).

46. The Wine CMO, with its strict linkage of quality with geographical indications, reflects and reinforces this mind-set. Nor, as we have observed in Chapter One, do we believe that the Commission's latest proposals will do much to correct it. The fundamental weakness is the continuing division of EU wines into 'sheep' and 'goats' (quality and table wines), which will remain even under the regime proposed by the Commission. Yet it is here where New World producers have found their main entry into the European market: they have exploited a wide gap in the market which has opened up between top-class GI-based wines, which are of interest to those who understand and appreciate them, and cheaper but appealing wines which are not officially regarded within the Community as being wines of quality. They have been able to do this because they have been responsive to changes in wine-drinking habits and consumer preferences.

47. New World producers also blend their wines to give consistency of taste. Jean-Louis Alaux, President of the Federation of Wine Producers of the Aude region of Languedoc-Roussillon (FVIA) referred to this difference between EU and New World wine-making:

> "If there is a difference in flavour, taste or aroma from one year to the next in other countries, they can inject this aroma. If there is a little bit of sun missing in California, they can inject an aroma to replace the missing sun, and we cannot do this in France ... Because we [FVIA] are avant-garde, we are looking to the future; we have been asking for a long

---

15 COPA-COGECA is the EU-wide representative organisation of wine producers and cooperatives

time to have the same opportunities in these terms as our competitors." (Q 787)

We had already heard from Michael Paul on the need for consistency of taste to appeal to the mass market. "If you are a purist and very seriously into wine", he told us, "the idea of vintage variation appeals—because wine becomes almost a lifelong study, and therefore vintage variation is something that is attractive ... If you are the average consumer, the last thing they want is vintage variation" (Q 516). And Luigi Polizzi took the view that "blending allows the wine maker to perform" (Q 534).

48. It is clear from the evidence we have received that many wine producers within Member States are alive to this fundamental change which has taken place in wine-drinking habits and in the attitudes of consumers towards wine. We are not however convinced that the reforms which the Commission has proposed will have any serious effect in reorienting the industry towards this changed market. The Commission states, in its Legislative Proposal, that "the concept of EU quality wines is based on a geographical origin approach" and that "the EU wants to confirm, adapt, promote and enhance this concept worldwide"[16]. The trouble is that increasingly the global market does not see it that way. In our view a more radical approach is needed—namely, to break the connection between quality and geography and to allow all EU wines to compete on their merits as viewed by consumers.

49. We do not wish to be misunderstood. As we have said in our earlier report, we have no difficulty at all with EU wines being produced and marketed under PGI or PDO arrangements: if a thriving market for such wines can be found, fair and good. We also fully recognise that the owners of recognised PGIs or PDOs must be given regulatory protection against impersonation of their products by others. Our quarrel is with the notion that only PGI or PDO wines can be considered to be quality wines and with the Commission's proposal[17] that the producers of such wines should be given increased control over the marketing of wines in their areas. Such attempts to swim against the tide of consumer choice risk sabotaging the recovery of the industry and its ability to compete with wines from outside the Community.

Structure of the Industry

50. The EU wine industry displays three features which in our view are impeding its competitiveness—it is fragmented, it is producer-dominated and there is a lack of connectivity between those who grow and produce wine and those who market and drink it. We deal with each of these in turn.

Fragmentation

51. According to Eva Corral of COPA-COGCA, 71 per cent of EU vineyards have an average surface area of 5 hectares (Q 218). "The characteristic of the European wine industry", she observed, "is that, contrary to third countries, there are not really big companies in Europe. Most of the wine is produced by the producers and marketed by their cooperatives" (Q 224). Ms Corral went on to pose the question: "Because of the structure of production in the European Union, is it logical to think we can fully compete with Australia,

---

16 COM(2007)372 Final, Section 3.1

17 COM(2007)372 Final, Section 3.1

where they have an average of 50 hectares against 5 hectares in the European Union?" (Q 233)

52. This overall picture, however, masks a number of national and regional variations. According to Jacky Bonotaux, Economic Specialist at the French Agriculture Ministry's Regional Office in Bordeaux, wine growing in the Gironde region of France has seen a move away from family estates to corporate entities. "Corporate entities now account for 70 per cent of the wine-producing vineyards", he told us, "the exact opposite of what happens in the rest of France, where it is still 70 per cent family" (Q 863). The UK's own wine industry, though small, is growing rapidly and in a manner which is different from much of the EU. We were told by the UK Vineyards Association that the average size of a commercial vineyard in Britain was already around 35 acres[18] and that the figure was increasing towards 100 acres[19]. Robert Lindo, the Association's Chairman, described the average UK holding as "vast for the EU but small compared to places like Australia", where (he suggested) 150 acres was thought to be the minimum viable size for a commercial operation (QQ 563–564).

53. Much of the situation in Continental Europe derives from historical factors, in particular the handing down of vineyards from one generation to the next as distinct from vineyards being taken over progressively by larger enterprises. Michael Paul believed that this was a factor of the industry's lack of competitiveness. "If you are a family company", he commented, "your main objective is maybe to hand this over to your son or it may be that you just want to make great wine. The idea of making a return on investment and having a business plan ... actually does not exist" (Q 536). Jean-Louis Alaux, in Languedoc-Roussillon, saw another problem. "In generations past", he told us, "children have inherited their family estates but this inheritance does not necessarily mean that the skills have been learned along with the inheritance" (Q 767).

54. According to Michael Paul, the Wine CMO itself could be compounding the problems of an industry which is fragmented into thousands of small producers. Commenting on the difference in scale of Australian and EU vineyards, he observed: "The whole culture and ethos of wine-making is going to be different if you have an almost infinite amount of land to expand into. You could be a very, very go-ahead producer of Burgundy, but actually there is not much you can do other than, perhaps, make better and better wine, if you cannot get more land" (Q 518). While Mr Paul's statement may seem at first sight to be self-evident, it assumes a deeper significance when viewed against the Commission's proposal to extend the ban on new plantings from 2010 to 2013, not to mention the pressure from some quarters to have it extended still further. We have already argued that, with the ending of subsidised distillation, there is no need for a ban on new plantings and that such a prohibition will serve only to protect inefficient wine producers and to keep more enterprising growers out of the market. It will also help to reinforce the fragmented nature of the European wine industry and hinder its ability to compete with imports from New World countries.

---

18 Equivalent to 14 hectares

19 Equivalent to 40 hectares

Producer Domination

55. Philip Gregan, Chief Executive Officer of New Zealand Winegrowers, took the view that the focus of the EU wine industry was on production. "It is not about the market", he told us. "It is saying: 'This is how we are going to produce wine, these are the controls we are going to put in place, and then you, the market, you have to take what we give you'. The market has not liked it; it has moved away" (Q 737).

56. Are such scathing criticisms well founded? During our visit to Bordeaux, we took evidence from Claude Mailleau, Area Director of the French Ministry of Agriculture. Mr Mailleau described to us how 'quality' wine growing in the Bordeaux region was managed:

> "Bordeaux and its vineyards are almost exclusively AOC[20] wines. We have a total of fifty seven. That forms a triangle, in decreasing order of prestige and reputation, from the top six—like St-Emilion and Margaux—down to the bottom of the triangle, the simple *Appellation* of Bordeaux. Within that you have the wine syndicates, or wine guilds, whose job is to define and propose particular levels of yield, the number of hectolitres per hectare for each harvest, which is then ratified by the INAO[21]. That gives you some idea of the complexity of the structure, it being a profession that is essentially driven by those involved within the profession, the growers, but under the control of the relevant ministries" (Q 863).

57. How, we wondered, was the market involved in the process? Mr Mailleau drew our attention to the CIVB, whose role he described to us as being "to ensure the development and the promotion of the vineyards" and whose evidence to us suggests that it is well seized of the need for reform of the wine sector. But, said Mr Mailleau, CIVB "are not there for policy-making; policy-making is on a national scale" (Q 863). It would be difficult to find a better illustration of what is wrong with the industry: it exists primarily for its producers.

58. Nor in our view do the Commission's proposals hold out much hope for change. We acknowledge that the removal of subsidies for distillation will act as a spur to competitiveness and we are clear that, without this particular change, reform of the wine sector would be doomed. Nonetheless there are a number of aspects of the Commission's proposals which seem to us to perpetuate the existing producer focus of the Wine CMO. The proposals include, for example, the right of Member States to "classify which wine grape varieties may be planted, replanted or grafted on their territories" and a requirement on Member States not to allow specified grape varieties to be grown within their borders[22]. Member States are also to be given "competences" to restrict new plantings, even after the lifting of the current planting ban, in areas producing PGI ore PDO wines[23]. While we recognise that arguments might be advanced to justify such proposals individually, we are concerned about the mind-set which underlies many of them—that the

---

20 Appellation d'Origine Controllee

21 Institut Nationale d'Appellations d'Origine

22 COM(2007)372 Final, Article 18

23 COM(2007)372 Final, Section 3.1

industry should be regulated by administrative fiat rather than be left to respond to market pressures.

59. Philip Gregan believed that "what Europe has to do is to move from basing its regulatory model on assisting producers to a regulatory model which is based on facilitating a comprehensive market place" (Q 744). Alain Vironneau, President of CIVB, said much the same thing. During our visit to Bordeaux he told us that "Europe needs to have the same facilities and tools as the rest of the competition ... [It] has to take on board the realities and create a situation whereby there are genuine criteria adapted to the change in consumption and not just pinned to the producer and his vines" (Q 806).

Connectivity

60. Lars Hoelgaard, Deputy Director-General for Agriculture at the European Commission, saw the need for "more integration between producers and the selling of the product, which is one of the areas where many of our stakeholders are saying there is a lack of integration, a lack of coherence, and there is a need to reinforce the whole chain" (Q 309). Lene Naesager, the Member of the Agriculture Commissioner's cabinet with responsibility for wine reform, put it rather more directly. There was a need, she said:

> "to become more competitive and to start thinking differently, so that they do not think: 'Now I am producing the wine because I like to produce my wine like that'. They need to think about what does the consumer outside France—for example, in Denmark or in the UK—want to drink. They really lack awareness, the wine producers today. They are only thinking about producing their own wines. They do not think: 'How do I really sell my wine? How do I persuade people that they should drink my wine?'" (Q 345)

61. This is not, however, just a matter of producer conservatism. Part of the problem lies in the fragmented nature of the industry which makes it difficult for the thousands of small EU producers to get a clear vision of what the market wants and to form robust links with wine retailers. Julian Dyer, for Sainsburys, referred to the smaller supply base with which he had to deal in Australia and California in contrast to the complexity of the EU wine industry (Q 650). Dan Jago, speaking for Tesco, told us:

> "The European market is pretty much family and dynastic: the New World is corporate and large and, therefore, has found the ability to deal with retailers on a much more professional level perhaps than some relationship-driven styles of the Older World" (Q 671).

62. It is here where there needs to be better coordination between what the industry can provide and what the market can sell. It is not so much that producers are not interested in making wine which is marketable as that many of them appear to be unaware of what the consumer is willing to buy. The problem is perhaps most acute among those small-scale producers who grow grapes and deliver them to cooperatives—and who, as Alain Vironneau told us in Bordeaux, have no contact with the market (Q 796). There is a clear role here for wine trade associations and cooperatives to explore the market and to feed back the intelligence they acquire to the producer in the vineyard. Eva Corral, of COPA-COGECA, recognised this need and wished to see a "market observatory" established to monitor changes in consumer demand and communicate these to growers. And Julian Dyer too was clear

about the important role of trade groups. "Some of the trade bodies from the New World", he said, "have been extremely dynamic and unified in terms of uniting industry to understand what the customers want and assisting the producers to develop that" (Q 667).

63. The Commission is proposing that around a tenth of the current Wine CMO budget should be devoted to 'promotion'. Its Explanatory Memorandum refers to "making the consumer better informed about European wines"[24]. This in our view is a most telling phrase. While we applaud the Commission's objective—to increase the sale of EU-produced wines—we believe that the strategy which is proposed needs to be turned on its head. We should be thinking in terms of making the EU producer better informed about consumers' tastes rather than making consumers better informed of what the industry has to offer. In a word, the starting point for any campaign of promotion should be the consumer, not the producer.

Impact of Reform

64. In the course of our inquiry we have encountered a number of concerns about the impact of reform of the EU wine sector. There is concern about the effect of some of the proposed measures, in particular the withdrawal of distillation subsidies and the grubbing-up of vineyards, on the social and economic fabric of wine-producing regions. There is also concern, sometimes overt in relation to the Commission's proposals on wine-making practices but latent in other areas, lest the introduction of a more commercial approach to wine production might undermine the culture of the industry and result in EU wine becoming just another beverage with mass consumer appeal. And we have encountered some concern over the possible environmental impact of a reduction of wine-growing in some regions of the Community. These are understandable concerns on the part of an old-established industry which is being brought face to face with the hard realities of a global market. In this section we attempt to explore them and to assess how justified they are.

Social and Economic Impact

65. Eva Corral emphasised to us the labour-intensive nature of much of the EU wine industry. She believed that two and a half million jobs were linked to the harvesting of grapes and suggested to us that a large part of the economy of wine-producing areas depended on wine. "We have to be very careful", Ms Corral concluded, "about the way we do our reform" (Q 218). Reforming the wine sector, particularly the proposed withdrawal of subsidies for distillation, is bound to have an impact which will affect not only wine producers themselves but also other parts of the rural economy. Claude Mailleau reminded us that in the Bordeaux region there was much rural activity, including tourism, shops and crafts, which revolved around the wine sector (QQ 864, 884). All this has to be taken into account in assessing the impact of reform on local communities.

66. Care must be taken, however, not to exaggerate the effects of reform. We have drawn attention in our earlier report[25] to evidence given to us by the French Agriculture Ministry that a high proportion of wine-growing concerns

---

24 COM(2007)372 Final, Section 3.4

25 See HL 144, Part I, Paragraph 80

in Languedoc-Roussillon were run by people who had other jobs and who were keeping alive small inherited vineyards as a sideline activity. French wine-growers are not unique in this respect. Zoltan Somogyi, Hungarian SCA spokesman, told us that, though there were 130,000 registered wine growers in Hungary, only 12,000 of them were producing wine for the market. Many of them worked at their vines as a hobby: Mr Somogyi gave us the example of a railway employee who tended his vineyard after work. He did not believe that giving up wine growing would have a significant impact on the everyday lives of many of those concerned (QQ 364, 377). The picture is not, of course, a homogeneous one across the Community. As we have already remarked, there are areas—such as the Gironde region of France—where substantial consolidation of vineyards has taken place and where those who produce wine do so as their sole or main activity (QQ 824, 862, 864). Nonetheless, it is fair to say that the crude numbers of people involved in wine-growing do not by any means tell the whole story: it is necessary to consider the structure of the industry as well.

67. It is also necessary to take a medium-to-long term view of wine sector reform rather than to focus exclusively on its short-term impact. Distillation subsidies and other market intervention measures address the symptoms rather than deal with the underlying cause of the malaise, which is the inadequate market focus and lack of competitiveness of much of the wine sector. It seems to us that the industry is in many respects in an analogous position to a patient whose symptoms are being relieved by palliatives but who is reluctant to undergo surgery to remove the cause of the illness. As with the sick patient, the wine sector will undoubtedly experience short-term pain when curing the malady replaces palliation of its symptoms. But in the longer term the industry will be stronger and, as it begins to attract new markets, it will be able to expand again.

68. For these reasons we are in no doubt that the Commission's proposals, considered as a package, are sound and that, if they are accepted, they could well set the industry, after a period of recovery, on the road to greater vitality and growth. We fully understand the reluctance of some parts of the industry to undergo the prescribed treatment, but we are convinced that it is necessary and that the measures proposed by the Commission to ease the pain of the transition to a new Wine CMO will be sufficient to alleviate the upheaval and hardship which some may suffer. There are generous retirement grants on offer to those who cease wine growing, compensation for vines which are grubbed up, aid for restructuring of existing enterprises and rural development funding to help diversify employment in wine-growing regions. As a result this is a relatively pain-free package. If it is not accepted, the position of the industry vis-à-vis its non-EU competitors will only worsen and the impact of postponed reform will only be more severe.

Cultural Impact

69. We turn now to a wider issue—the impact of reform on the culture of European wine production. There are some strands to this issue on which we have already commented, including the proposed EU-wide recognition of oenological practices endorsed by the *Organisation Internationale Des Vins*, the use of sucrose to enrich wine and the blending of wine to produce consistency of taste from one year to the next. Underlying all of them, however, is a concern lest reform of the wine sector should lead to an old-established craft industry being turned into a vehicle of mass production.

70. Eva Corral was concerned that reform, while necessary, should not lead to EU wine producers simply copying New World business and oenological methods and having "a product that has no identity" (QQ 241, 242). That identity, she believed, was bound up closely with the definition of wine as a natural product. "It is made by producers", she said, "it is regulated by the Common Agricultural Policy, so it is an agricultural product" (Q 232). On these grounds Ms Corral did not favour the blending of wines to achieve year-on-year consistency of taste:

> "The case now is that we have big companies that have vines in a number of continents and they put them together and mix them, so that they can get the same flavour every year and have a standard product, whereas our concept of the product and its characteristics is that we cannot do that" (Q 235).

71. Lars Hoelgaard, of the European Commission, underlined these concerns when he drew our attention to concerns that EU oenological techniques should not be undermined by bilateral agreements with third countries. He told us that there was a desire in some quarters that the wine which was consumed in the EU should be made on the basis of "good, old, traditional practices". He added:

> "There is very little of that approach in non-producing, wine-consuming Member States, like the UK, Denmark, Norway, Sweden, Ireland and others, who have no particular adherence to the culture compared to those who come from wine-producing countries, who have a very strong relation to that" (Q 311).

72. David Statham, of the UK Food Standards Agency (FSA), drew a parallel, in the context of wine enrichment, between the production of wine and milk. "We used to have a situation", he said, "where you could not adjust the fat content and the water content of milk; you had to have a specific level, because that is what naturally came from the cow". The Wine CMO's attitude to wine enrichment was, he believed, similar. "What it is ... saying is that we can only produce wine in the natural way as opposed to producing wine in a way that has the alcohol level correctly worked out ... There is only one traditional way of doing this, in the way that there probably was only one traditional way of milking your cow" (Q 104). Sarah Appleby, of the FSA, summed it up with the question: "What makes a wine a wine? Is it because it has gone through a traditional process? Or is it a composite product with the addition of alcohol to some fruit base" (Q 106).

73. In our earlier report we quoted Philip Gregan as saying that the EU attitude to wine production, and in particular the linking of wine quality with the concept of *terroir*, contained "flawed theology" (Q 707). These may perhaps seem harsh words. But it is fair to say that, in taking evidence during our inquiry, we have found that attitudes to reform of the EU wine sector sometimes migrate from the socio-economic and take on a cultural flavour, as if reform is associated by some with advancing philistinism. While we understand the concerns which are felt in some quarters, we do not believe that reform will have the dire consequences which appear to be foreseen. We concur with the view of New Zealand Winegrowers that "being consumer-led does not mean that wine will inevitably become a commodity catering to the lowest common denominator. In fact, the international wine market is highly

sophisticated and there is strong consumer demand for products at all quality levels"[26].

74. The Commission is not, in any case, suggesting that traditional wine-making practices should be abandoned. Indeed, while it is proposed that some oenological techniques which are approved by the OIV but currently banned within the EU should be allowed, other proposals—for example, on the use of sucrose—are more restrictive than the status quo. EU wine-makers who wish to continue to use traditional practices will be free to do so and, if they can find a market for wines produced in this way, they will no doubt continue as they have done. Perhaps the real cause of concern, however, is that, with distillation subsidies removed, traditional wine-makers who cannot find a market for their products may have to modify their products, by adapting them to consumer demand, in order to do so. Understandable as such concerns may be, the current regime, with its heavy reliance on distillation subsidies and its over-restrictive network of regulations, cannot be allowed to continue.

Environmental Impact

75. Finally, we turn to the environmental impact of reform. Giuseppe Castiglione, the Member of the European Parliament designated as *Rapporteur* for the Commission's Proposal, suggested to us that "in many parts of Europe, if there were no more vineyards, from the environmental point of view it would be a real catastrophe" (Q 266). On the other hand, Emmanuel Jacquin, Head of the Wine Reform Unit at the European Commission, told us that there were environmental drawbacks as well as advantages from wine-growing, stemming from the use of pesticides and erosion. Dietrich Guth, German SCA representative, underlined these problems. "Maybe the effect [of reducing wine growing] on the environment will be even better", he suggested, "because we are using a huge amount of pesticides in those regions or, if you look at wine production in Germany in the valleys and the hills, there we have a problem of soil erosion" (Q 463).

76. The Commission's plan is to use the Single Farm Payment to safeguard the environment where vineyards are grubbed up. In Emmanuel Jacquin's words:

> "We want to improve the positive side of the environmental benefits brought by vineyards by introducing environmental conditions and by using cross-compliance more and more … When the vineyards ask to be grubbed up, we can check whether this will cause environmental damage and we can oblige the farmers to respect a certain number of conditions to ensure that we take care of the soil. The main instrument that we will use for this is to grant a Single Farm Payment to the grubbed-up area so that it will become automatically subject to cross-compliance for the whole farm, even if the farmer has only grubbed up one hectare" (Q 321).

Moreover, the Commission's proposal states that, "to avoid social and/or environmental problems, Member States will be allowed to limit grubbing-up in mountains and steep slopes vineyards as well as in regions under specific environmental constraints"[27]. And the proposed transfer of funds

26 HL 144, Part II, Page 174

27 COM(2007)372 Final, Section 3.6

from Pillar I (Wine CMO) to Pillar II (Rural Development) includes "agri-environment support to cover additional costs and income foregone in providing and maintaining vinescapes/cultural landscapes"[28].

77. Against this background we do not believe that there need be serious cause for concern as regards the environmental consequences of reform, although the practical impact of cross compliance measures will need to be monitored closely.

28 COM(2007)372 Final, Section 3.3

CHAPTER 3: CONCLUSIONS

78. In this concluding report we have sought to do two things—to re-examine, in the light of evidence from HM Government, our preliminary findings on the Commission's Legislative Proposal; and to draw attention to some key characteristics of the European wine industry which will need to change if a new Wine CMO along the lines proposed by the Commission is to produce real results. In this chapter we address the same two subjects in reverse order. First, we attempt to pull together our thoughts on the EU wine industry and then we set out our final conclusions on the Commission's proposals.

The EU Wine Industry

79. The key objective of reform must be to stimulate a greater sense of competitiveness in many parts of the wine industry. Competitiveness, however, is one of those qualities, like virtue, to which everyone subscribes in principle while having differing views as to what it means in practice. Giusseppe Castiglione took the view that "it is absolutely necessary to give new impetus … to the European wine-growing companies facing these new challenges from countries which more and more are finding outlets in the European market for their wines, and it is something we have to face up to. We have to try and get new market share via reform". He thought the answer to the problem was more promotion of EU wines:

> "The competitiveness of our undertakings can be made more profitable with sustained support for marketing. Our competitors, we have noted, really have massive advertising campaigns, even if their products are of lesser quality, are less good for the environment or less linked to the structure of the land. Nevertheless a tremendous amount of investment goes into the advertisements, certainly compared to what we are doing as Europeans" (Q 266).

80. Lene Naesager agreed about the need to direct reform at increasing market share. She supported increased promotion, but she also took the view that other measures were needed too:

> "We need to look at the different tools that we have now and we believe that the combination of the different tools will lead to better competitiveness for EU wines. For instance, if we look at the money that is now being used for distillation, that is not a very positive measure, using money to distil the wine that we produce. That is one of the reasons why we want to use the money better. It is one of the reasons why we have created 'national envelopes'" (Q 309).

81. Such initiatives—promotion, grubbing-up, restructuring, cross compliance—are all very well in their own right and we support them as stepping stones towards a more vigorous and profitable wine industry. They are, however, all administrative measures and, as such, they will have only limited success if there is not a more fundamental change in the outlook of those working at the coalface. There is in our view a need to move from the mind-set of an industry which, in some sectors at least, thinks in terms of wine quality as something apart from the consumer and from a structure which is fragmented both horizontally (with thousands of very small vineyards under family control) and vertically (with slender connection between those who

grow the grapes, make the wine and sell the finished product). Julian Dyer offered this advice for getting the EU wine industry moving again:

> "Be more open-minded. Take a look above the parapet and see what else is out there. Really understand what customers are drinking. Produce modern styles of wine that are in tune with today's palate. Be competitive on price. Work collaboratively as an industry. Those industries that do well work together. Australia is a great example: it is one industry; they are in it together. In France, Italy, Spain, it is each against the other" (Q 678).

82. Small producers will always have difficulty surviving in an open market. Their survival depends on injections of funds unconnected with wine production, whether from personal income or public funds. The only market-oriented solution to this is to secure greater scale of production, whether from corporate or cooperative farming. Understandable as is the desire to maintain small-scale production, the plain fact is that such a structure is not economically viable in a global wine market and with changed attitudes to wine consumption. If persisted in, the consequence will inevitably be that the industry will continue to lose market share. Subsidies from public funds may palliate the situation but they will not solve the problem or make the industry more competitive. What is needed, therefore, is greater cooperation within the industry, and in our view this must be led by the marketers, as the people in touch with consumer demand, rather than the producers. Setting up such networks would, we believe, be a worthwhile use of wine CMO funds via national envelopes.

Conclusions

83. Our final conclusions as regards the Commission's Legislative Proposal are therefore as follows:

Distillation

(a) We concur with the Government's view that the ending of subsidised distillation is a *sine qua non* of reform of the wine sector. While most of the other measures proposed by the Commission are to be welcomed, the ending of subsidies for distillation is crucial to the success of the reform package as a whole. Without it, none of the other measures will be able to deliver the efficiency gains which are necessary to set the industry on its feet again. We therefore confirm our strong support for this proposal (Paragraph 7).

National Envelopes

(b) We confirm our acceptance of the concept of national envelopes. While an allocation formula for national envelopes which gives priority to the main wine-producing States is acceptable in the short term, the medium term aim should be to reduce wine sector funding overall and to re-assess the allocation of national envelopes among Member States (Paragraph 10).

(c) We support the Government's view regarding the usage of national envelopes—that they should be used for purposes which will promote the efficiency of the wine sector or address the consequences of its reform and that the most suitable way of achieving this is via transfer of funds from Pillar I to Pillar II of the CAP. For this reason we do not support the inclusion of 'Green Harvest' among eligible measures for funding from national envelopes and we confirm our opposition to this proposal (Paragraph 14).

Grubbing-Up

(d) We confirm our support for a programme of voluntary grubbing-up of uncompetitive vineyards and we reiterate our wish to see tight definition of the exemptions which Member States may invoke to block grubbing-up applications by wine growers (Paragraph 16).

The Ban on New Plantings

(e) We are pleased to see that the Government shares our view of the need to end the current planting ban. As regards the detail of this, we recognise that it is for the Government to make its own judgement of the situation, taking into account the concerns of the UK Wine Industry. However, it will be better for the EU wine industry as a whole if the ban is lifted sooner rather than later.

Enrichment

(f) We confirm our support for the ending of subsidies for the use of grape must in wine enrichment and our opposition to the proposed ban on the use of sucrose (Paragraph 23).

Rural Development

(g) We confirm our support for the transfer of a substantial proportion of Wine CMO funds from Pillar I to Pillar II of the CAP in order to support Rural Development programmes in wine-producing regions (Paragraph 25).

(h) We re-state our opposition to the use of Rural Development funds to remedy an economic problem resulting from a proposed administrative measure (banning the use of sucrose in wine enrichment) which makes no sense in its own right (Paragraph 28).

Wine Classification and Labelling

(i) We confirm our earlier view that, while the proposed relaxations in labelling rules are to be welcomed, the proposed new wine classification system is unlikely to be sufficient to reverse the trend of mass consumption of non-EU wines. We also wish to sound a note of concern lest the new system could be used to prevent entrepreneurial new wine makers from entering the market after the ending of the current planting ban (Paragraph 33).

Wine Making Practices

(j) We confirm our earlier support for the Commission's proposal that OIV-recommended oenological techniques should become the benchmark for authorisation of wine-making practices within the EU (Paragraph 34).

Single Farm Payment

(k) While we consider there would be advantage in bringing all land producing food and drink, including vineyards, within the Single Farm Payment system, we nonetheless support the more modest reform of bringing grubbed-up vineyard land within the ambit of the SFP (Paragraph 36).

84. In short, a new Wine CMO must be seen by the industry as something to help it to become competitive rather than, as has been the case in the past, as a vehicle on which to ride. No CMO can, of itself, make the industry competitive or save it from yet further loss of market share if the right attitudes are not present on the ground. Most of the various measures within the Commission's Legislative Proposal are capable, given realistic and constructive application by Member States and the industry, of turning the EU wine sector round and pointing it towards a brighter future. The new CMO must, however, be seen for what it is: a facilitating mechanism rather than a support structure, enabling the industry to move from its present reliance on subsidies to self-sufficiency in the market place.

APPENDIX 1: SUB-COMMITTEE D (ENVIRONMENT AND AGRICULTURE)

Sub-Committee D

The members of the Sub-Committee which conducted this inquiry were:-

Lord Bach
Viscount Brookeborough
Lord Cameron of Dillington
Lord Greaves
Baroness Jones of Whitchurch
Baroness Miller of Chilthorne Domer
Lord Moynihan
Lord Palmer
Lord Plumb
Lord Sewel (Chairman)
Viscount Ullswater

Declarations of Interest

A full list of Members' interests can be found in the Register of Lords Interests:

http://www.publications.parliament.uk/pa/ld/ldreg.htm

APPENDIX 2: LIST OF WITNESSES

The following witnesses gave evidence. Those marked * gave oral evidence.

* The Lord Rooker and Robin Manning, Department for Environment, Food and Rural Affairs

APPENDIX 3: A BRIEF GUIDE TO THE EU WINE SECTOR

This Appendix reproduces Chapter I of HL 144-I (Session 2006–2007), which describes the main features of the current regulations governing the production and marketing of EU wines. The text of that chapter is as follows:

Introduction

1. The European Union produces 60 per cent of the world's wine, more than four fifths of it being produced in three Member States—France, Italy and Spain. The EU is also the world's largest exporter of wine, with over €15 billion worth of exports annually. Across the Community, the wine sector provides employment for around one and a half million people—some 15 per cent of the agricultural workforce. This overall figure, however, masks significant national and regional variations. For example, half of all those employed in wine-growing are to be found in two Member States—Italy and Portugal; while in the French region of Languedoc/Roussillon nearly half of the agricultural workforce is engaged in wine-growing. At the other end of the scale, the UK wine industry employs no more than about 1,000 people, though wine-growing is a thriving industry in Britain.

2. Wine consumption is on the increase in some parts of the EU, including Britain. Within the Community as a whole, however, and especially in those Member States where most EU wine is produced, demand has fallen. Moreover, while exports of wine to non-Member States have been steadily rising and are generally healthy, imports to the Community from so-called New World countries (in particular, the United States, Australia, South Africa and Chile) have been rising more sharply in recent years and are now almost on a level with exports. This, together with a succession of good wine harvests, has resulted, in four out of the last six years, in a significant surplus of wine produced in the EU. These trends are illustrated in the chart at Figure 1:

FIGURE 1

Wine—Supply/Demand and Import/Exports

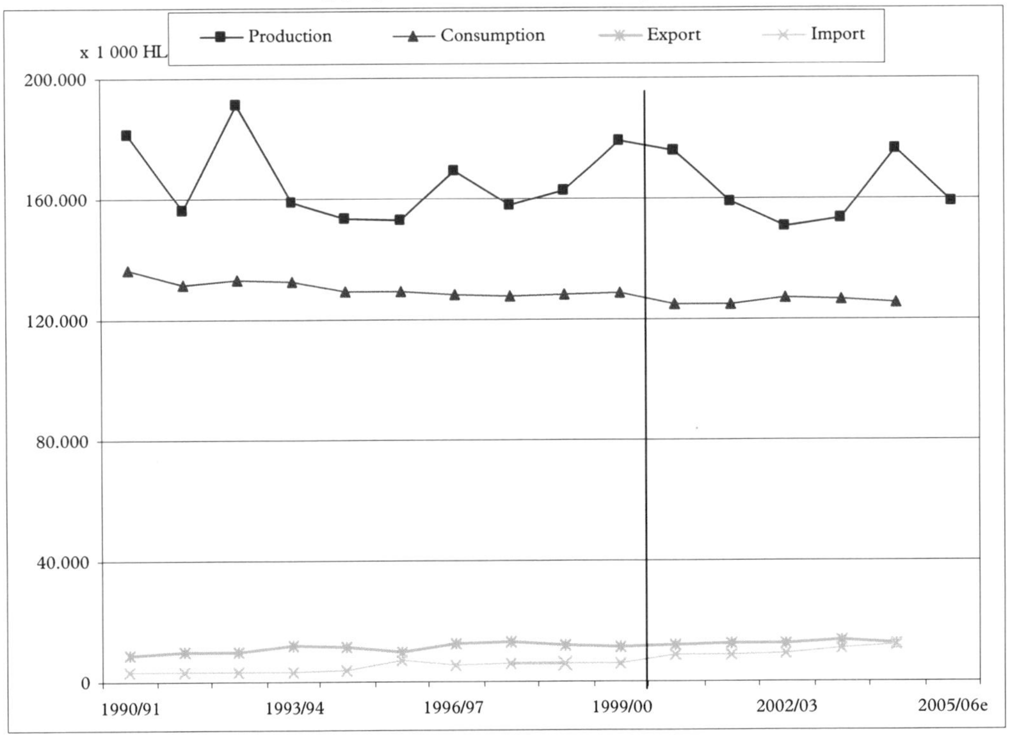

As a result market intervention measures have been activated under the terms of the Community's Common Market Organisation in Wine (the Wine CMO). These intervention measures, the rules for which were last revised in 1999, were designed to ensure market stability between years of good and poor harvests. It is now becoming clear, however, that the recurrent surpluses have deeper structural causes and it is argued in some quarters that the Wine CMO itself, with its system of subsidies and regulations, is a major factor of the current malaise.

3. In 2006, therefore, the European Commission launched a consultative process leading to the issue, in June of that year, of a Communication[29] entitled "Towards a Sustainable European Wine Sector". This set out a number of options for reform and commended one of them (described as "profound reform") for consideration. The Commission's Communication provided the starting point for our inquiry, in the course of which we have taken evidence from the Government, the European Parliament and Commission, a number of Member States and EU-wide organisations representing wine producers and traders. We have also received an external perspective of the EU wine regime from the Australian and New Zealand wine industries and a commercial assessment from two leading British supermarkets. Finally, we have visited two major wine-producing regions—Languedoc/Roussillon and Bordeaux—in order to see at first hand the challenges and opportunities of wine production in the EU and to hear the views of local wine-growers and regional development bodies. All the evidence collected in the course of our inquiry can be seen in Volume II.

4. In July 2007 the Commission published a Legislative Proposal[30] containing specific measures for reform. This Proposal is the main focus of our report. But, before we can come to consider it, it is necessary to explore what the current wine regime is and how it operates. That is the purpose of this Chapter.

The Existing Regime in Outline

5. The Common Agricultural Policy (CAP) contains a number of Common Market Organisations (CMOs) which set out the rules for the operation of particular sectors of the agriculture industry. Wine growing, production and marketing is just one of these. The first Wine CMO was established in 1962 and was geared to reconciling different oenological practices and wine-producing strategies among the six Member States of the then European Economic Community. The CMO has been revised on a number of occasions since then, most recently in 1999, when it was reconstituted under Council Regulation (EC) No 1493/1999. It is important to note that the Wine CMO was not included in the CAP reforms introduced in 2003 and, therefore, the rules governing the EU wine industry remain essentially as set out in the 1999 Regulation.

6. The Regulation itself recognises that "the rules governing the common organisation of the market in wine are extremely complex"[31]. Broadly speaking, however, it may be said that the existing regime consists, on the one hand, of a range of subsidies to support the EU wine industry and, on the other, of a series of regulations to control the ways in which wine is produced and marketed. The 1999 Regulation contains detailed rules covering both the administration of the subsidies and a number of other aspects of the wine industry, including the planting of vineyards, wine-making practices and wine classification.

---

29 COM(2006)319 dated 22 June 2006

30 COM(2007) 372 Final

31 Council Regulation (EC) No 1493/1999 dated 17 May 1999, Recital 10

7. A recent European Commission Working Paper[32] described the Wine CMO as "one of the largest and most complex common market organisations". Within the compass of this short Chapter we can do no more than highlight its main features. Much of the Council Regulation is technical in nature. We will attempt therefore to explain the operation of the wine regime in layman's language, though we recognise that this may on occasion result in some unavoidable over-simplification. We consider below each of the main features of the CMO under the two principal headings of Subsidies and Regulations.

Subsidies

8. The actual cost of the subsidies in any one year depends on the volume of the harvest and the prevailing market situation. According to the European Commission[33], in 2005 total expenditure on the wine sector came to €1.27 billion, and we were told by Robin Manning, Head of the Cereals and Wine Branch at the Department for Environment, Food and Rural Affairs (Defra) that "the budget for 2007 has now been adjusted down to €1.4 billion" (Q 16). In other words, subsidies to the wine sector are costing EU taxpayers the equivalent of nearly £1 billion a year. We were also told by officials from Defra that the wine sector accounts for between 2.5 per cent and 5.5 per cent of the CAP budget each year (Q 16).

9. The subsidies provided for under the 1999 Regulation fall under three main headings: market intervention measures, including various forms of subsidised distillation to remove wine from the market; financial support for the restructuring of wine production to make it more competitive; and the provision of premiums for the grubbing-up of vineyards in order to reduce production capacity.

Distillation

10. Distillation involves the processing of wine in order to separate out the alcohol. Subsidies for distillation, together with the storage of distilled wine, cost the EU some €630 million a year and account for the major part of spending under the Wine CMO. According to the Commission's 2006 Working Paper, "the objective of wine distillation is to withdraw production surpluses from the market at a guaranteed minimum producer price"[34]. Since 2000 an average of some 10 per cent of wine production has been distilled with the aid of EU subsidies every year.

11. The 1999 Regulation provides for three main categories of subsidised distillation[35]. They are:

(a) Distillation of the by-products of wine (the marc and the lees) in order to protect the quality of wine by preventing the over-pressing of grapes;

(b) "Crisis" distillation, which is designed to remove pockets of surplus from the market in order to protect prices;

(c) Potable alcohol distillation, which supplies the spirits industry and producers of brandy and liqueurs with wine alcohol.

---

32 Wine Common Market Organisation, February 2006, Section 1

33 Commission Press Release 06/245 "EU Wine Reform: Background Information on the Wine Sector", 22 June 2006

34 Wine Common Market Organisation, February 2006, Section 2.6

35 There is a fourth category, known as dual purpose distillation, which is applied to wines (mainly from Charente) which are considered to have a dual purpose and which, beyond a certain quantity, must be distilled. Expenditure on this category is, however, small compared with the other three—around €25 million per annum.

Distillation of by-products ((a) above) is compulsory. Wine growers must surrender for distillation all by-products of wine-making and these must contain a minimum amount of alcohol: if they do not, wine has to be surrendered. According to the Commission, compulsory distillation of by-products costs between €200 million and €230 million a year. "Crisis" distillation (b) and distillation to supply the potable alcohol industry (c) are optional. They cost around €180 million and €250 million a year, respectively. EU subsidies comprise aid to distillers to compensate them for the guaranteed price paid to producers and storage costs. In addition to subsidies for distillation, there is also a substantial subsidy for the use of concentrated grape must in the enrichment of wine (see Paragraph 19 below)

Restructuring

12. The 1999 Regulation refers[36] to "wine-growing areas where production is not aligned to demand but where production could be better aligned through restructuring of vineyards by varietal conversion, relocation of vineyards or improvement of vineyard management techniques". Subsidies are available for this purpose, and in 2005 the funds spent in this way accounted for €446 million (35 per cent of Wine CMO spending). The purpose of the subsidies is to compensate wine growers for loss of earnings during a period of conversion and to make a contribution to the costs of implementing the measures concerned. Whether restructuring has been fully effective in bringing supply and demand into balance is another question—see, for example, Paragraph 68 below.

Grubbing-Up

13. To help bring supply and demand into balance, the 1999 Regulation offers premiums to farmers in certain regions who agree permanently to abandon wine-growing. The management and administration of such "grubbing-up" schemes rests with the Member States concerned. They are able to designate the regions where premiums are offered and to set the level of the compensation. In 2005 expenditure on grubbing-up amounted to €31 million (2 per cent of the wine sector budget). Substantial grubbing-up of EU vineyards took place in the 1980s and early 1990s, but the persistence of surpluses indicates that the process did not go far enough.

Regulations

14. The 1999 Regulation includes a ban until 2010 on the planting of new vines for wine production. This is seen as a logical corollary to the various other market support measures, such as distillation subsidies and subsidised grubbing-up. The ban applies, as do the grubbing-up subsidies, only to wine production in Member States whose total annual production of wine exceeds 25,000 hectolitres. The UK wine industry is currently operating just below this threshold, but at the current rate of growth UK wine growers could find themselves by 2010 within the ambit of this regulation.

15. Undoubtedly the most complex of the regulations under the present regime are those which are concerned with wine classification and labelling. The complexity derives to a large extent from the fact that the regulations divide EU wines into two main groups—quality wines and table wines. This dichotomy is important because the classification of a wine can determine its eligibility for

[36] Council Regulation No. 1493/1999, Recital 28

subsidies (most of the intervention measures apply only to table wines) and because it determines what may be written about the wine on the bottle label (for example, table wines may not show the year of vintage or the grape variety).

16. However, while the Wine CMO sets out the broad parameters for identifying quality wines, the responsibility for recognising and controlling wine quality within their borders rests with Member States. They are required to lay down specific rules concerning the regions in which quality wine may be produced, the vine varieties considered suitable, wine-growing and wine-making methods, minimum natural alcoholic strength and the maximum yield permitted per hectare. They are also responsible for recognising Geographical Indications (GIs), such as the French *Appellations d'Origine Controllees*, which may be used in the marketing of EU wine.

17. In these circumstances it is perhaps not surprising that there is considerable variation within the EU wine market as regards classification. According to the Commission[37], there are now over 10,000 EU wines marketed under a GI of one sort or another, some of which are highly regarded by wine experts while others are judged to be of indifferent quality. The labelling restrictions also pose difficulties for the marketing of some types of wines. The regulations do not apply to New World wine entering the EU. New World producers do not divide their wines into "quality" and "table" wines but tend to classify their wines by grape variety (e.g. Shiraz, Cabernet Sauvignon, Sauvignon Blanc) or brand name (e.g. Jacob's Creek, Turning Leaf) or, in some cases, region (e.g. Napa Valley). The current EU system of classifying wine into "sheep" and "goats" has undoubtedly been a factor of the penetration of New World wines into the Community market place. New World producers have, in effect, exploited a gap in the market by offering wine tailored to customer preferences, informatively labelled, at competitive prices and, in many cases, blended in order to guarantee consistency of taste. The Wine CMO's complex and restrictive regulations, however, make it difficult for EU producers to compete.

18. Yet another area of regulation under the 1999 CMO concerns the way in which wine is produced. The Regulation lays down a list of permitted oenological (wine-making) practices, including the type of grapes which may be used and the extent to which additives may be employed to enrich wine—i.e. to increase its natural alcoholic strength. There is, in fact, an international organisation—*Organisation Internationale des Vins (OIV)* (See Box 1)—of which most wine-producing countries[38] are members and which, as one of its functions, sets global wine-making standards and assesses and approves wine-making practices. The EU list of approved practices is, however, more restrictive than the OIV list, to which most New World wine producers adhere.

BOX 1

Organisation Internationale des Vins (OIV)

The OIV replaced the former International Vine and Wine Office in 2001. It is an inter-governmental scientific and technical body concerned with the production of wines. Its declared aims are to assist producers, consumers and others with technical information on wine and wine products and to contribute to international harmonisation of wine-making practices and standards. Its General Assembly adopts resolutions, normally by consensus, of a general, scientific, technical, economic or legal nature

---

37 Wine Common Market Organisation, February 2006, Section 2.4.1

38 Though not the UK

19. The detailed EU wine-making regulations are intended to take account of differing production conditions across the Community, in particular climate. Thus, for example, wine-growers in the North and Centre of the Community are permitted to increase alcoholic strength by more than are growers in the Mediterranean region, where the climate is such that little or no enrichment is considered to be required. Enrichment may be carried out by the use of either sucrose (beet or cane sugar) or concentrated grape must. Wine producers in the Mediterranean may use only the latter, but as this is significantly more expensive than sucrose a subsidy is made available from the Wine CMO with the aim of promoting a level economic playing field between growers in different areas. This subsidy currently costs some €156 million annually.

Summary

20. To sum up therefore, under the existing Wine CMO there are subsidies (in round figures) as follows:

Distillation (all forms)	€630 million
Grape Must	€150 million
Restructuring	€450 million
Grubbing-Up	€30 million
Total	€1,260 million

There is also a complex network of regulations dealing with the classification of wine and the rules for making it.

21. We make this report to the House for debate.

APPENDIX 4: RECENT REPORTS

Recent Reports from the Select Committee

Session 2006–07

Evidence from the Minister for Europe on the Outcome of the December European Council (4th Report, Session 2006–07, HL Paper 31)

Government Responses: Session 2004–05 (6th Report, Session 2006–07, HL Paper 38)

The Commission's 2007 Legislative and Work Programme (7th Report, Session 2006–07, HL Paper 42)

Evidence from the Ambassador of the Federal Republic of Germany on the German Presidency (10th Report, Session 2006–07, HL Paper 56)

Recent Reports prepared by Sub-Committee D (Environment and Agriculture)

Session 2006–2007

Water Framework Directive: Making It Work (27th Report Session 2006–2007, HL Paper 136)

European Wine: A Better Deal for All (30th Report Session 2006–2007, HL Paper 144)

Session 2005–2006

The Future Financing of the Common Agricultural Policy (2nd Report Session 2005–06, HL Paper 7)

European Union Fisheries Legislation (7th Report Session 2005–06, HL Paper 24)

The United Kingdom Presidency: Defra's Priorities, (12th Report Session 2005–06, HL Paper 36)

Too much or too little? Changes to the EU Sugar Regime (18th Report Session 2005–06, HL Paper 80-I and 80-II)

Managing nuclear safety and waste: the role of the EU (37th Report Session 2005–06, HL Paper 211-I and 211-II)

The EU Strategy on Biofuels: from field to fuel (47th Report Session 2005–2006, HL Paper 267-I and 267-II)

WEDNESDAY 25 JULY 2007

Present		
Present	Bach, L Jones of Whitchurch, B Moynihan, L Palmer, L	Plumb, L Sewel, L (Chairman) Ullswater, V

Examination of Witnesses

Witnesses: LORD ROOKER, a Member of the House, Minister of State for Sustainable Farming and Food, and MR ROBIN MANNING, Head of Wine and Cereals Branch, Department for Environment, Food and Rural Affairs, examined.

Q906 ***Chairman:*** Thank you very much, Minister, for coming along. It is always a delight to have you before this Committee. It is good value for money—which is more than can be said for the wine regime! This is a formal session; the evidence is being taken and you will get the transcript and be able to have a look. I wonder if we could start, really, by inviting you to give us your general overview of where we are on the wine reform, which bits you support in the Commission's proposals, which bits you query and where you think the difficulties are going to be—in about 30 seconds.

Lord Rooker: Can I say at the outset we think the Commission's proposals are very positive. I have to say, looking at the summary of your interim report's conclusions—13 of them—that in principle we agree with all of them. There are probably a couple of them to a lesser or greater extent, so we are on the same track. We think they have been very bold. There are some very strong points, really: to get rid of all this artificial market support and try and get, if you like, the French, the Spanish and the Italians to grow up and realise they are in a market with customers and not, therefore, the producer. There are some areas of concern, of course. I suppose, in some ways—it is not "nimbyism"—there are two areas of concern as far as the English wine industry is concerned, which, of course, is the issue of the enrichment and the issue of the ban on the planting of vines. By and large, we think they are very bold and we want to give them maximum support for the issues that are really serious—i.e. that artificial market support should cease. In doing that, I have to say in conclusion that we will have to negotiate, maybe, some areas in order to achieve our overall objective to support the Commission. We are going to have to give on a few things, probably.

Q907 ***Chairman:*** Where do you think the real difficulties are going to be for the Commission?

Lord Rooker: Frankly—and Robin can give you a more stark update than myself—if it was up to some of the Member States, I have to say, the Commission would not be doing anything anyway. Let us get this clear: some of the Member States do not want to move; they are living in the past. They would like to carry on with all the market support to control over who can grub-up and who cannot, to do things on labels that are still meaningless to consumers while allowing the competition from the New World to sweep the board. So it is going to be very difficult. In fact, if you take the planting ban, for example, which is due to lift in 2010 but there is a rearguard action is extend it to 2013, the English system is planned on 2010 not 2013 but they want that extended; 2013 is no good for them. That is a sticking point. We will support the Commission root and branch—and vine, if I can put it that way—on that. That is important. We want to get out of that, if we can, get an uplift of the 25,000 hectore-litre limit, because obviously we are not included in the ban because of our production, but we are getting close to the limit, as you appreciate.

Chairman: I wonder if we could go to the critical point of distillation.

Q908 ***Lord Moynihan:*** My Lord Chairman, I will keep my question very short to assist the Minister. The Commission, as you know, Minister, has proposed the ending of all subsidised distillation. Are you content that no scope has been left for similar subsidies to be reintroduced through the back door—for example, through the "crisis management" and "green harvest" measures provided for in the national envelopes?

Lord Rooker: We want to avoid that. Certainly, as far as the distillation is concerned, it has had virtually no effect on production. They have just carried on producing. You cannot think of a less value-for-money arrangement—it is taxpayers' money, let us face it. The green harvest would be a way through if they do something to destroy the grapes, if you like, or pick them and destroy them before they make the wine that has to be distilled. That would be an advantage in some ways; you have stopped doing some of the process. However, we wish to avoid back door subsidies. We must not give them a route that still encourages them to over-produce, which is the issue here. The immediate abolition of distillation is something that is a sticking point for us because it is that which brings in the culture change for the rest—

Q909 *Chairman:* In a way, if you just did the distillation that would affect everything else, would it not?
Lord Rooker: Yes, it would.

Q910 *Lord Moynihan:* Fighting back-door subsidies in the negotiations is an issue that is coming up, I assume, at the moment?
Mr Manning: Absolutely. There is quite a lot of scepticism around the Commission, on the one hand, saying that they are going to abolish all subsidies but, at the same time, provide an opportunity, maybe, for Member States to have a green harvest scheme, because the green harvest scheme is a form of market support. I think it is fair to say that it is probably less damaging than the support systems we have at the moment, which are encouraging wine to be produced, so you go through the process of producing wine only for that to distort the market and then very expensive measures have to be introduced in order to clear the market ready for next year's harvest. So the green harvest is a less distortive way of dealing with that. We certainly believe that it should not form part of the regime for ever and a day, and it is, of course, optional on Member States whether or not they wish to introduce a green harvest scheme. It is one of the closed menu of measures that they can introduce, and it was quite informative that on Day Two of the Working Group the Cypriots said that they ran a green harvesting scheme in 2002, I think it was, before they joined the community, and based on their experience of running a scheme like that they would not recommend it to any other Member State because it is just so difficult to control to make sure that it is done properly. In terms of market impact it had very limited impact whatsoever. We need to see the National Envelopes being a suite of things which Member States may choose or not choose to introduce, but I do not think, at the end of the day, it will have a major impact on the situation. The most important thing, as we have already said, is that from Day One the lifeblood of the uncompetitive industry is withdrawn so they have to face market reality because distillation goes.

Q911 *Viscount Ullswater:* Of course, we have touched on national envelopes. Most of the money is going to be allocated to the national envelopes. I would like to have your comments on the proposed formula for dividing this up between the Member States. Do you feel that the Commission will be able to hold on to its criteria for the use of the money in the national envelopes? Or do you think that, once it gets into the Member States' hands, they will just do exactly what they want with it? I know that the Commission want to try and hold on to the criteria but in negotiation I wonder whether they are going to be able to hang on to that. If there is another formula that you think would work? Could you suggest one?
Lord Rooker: First of all, we support the concept of the national envelopes, and there is an inevitability as I hinted at in my opening remarks—the three major producers have had most of the money and that will probably continue while we go through a transitional period. Robin explained to me this morning some of the mystique about the formula and some of the figures that we do not know as well, in the sense that we do not know the precise way that things will be carved up. It is quite clear, on what figures we have seen, that France, Italy and Spain will be the recipients of most of the support, however that is driven through the system. I think that is something we have got to live with because it is part of the price of stopping the thing we have just touched on, of the crude market support of distillation. That is part of where we are going to have to negotiate, I think. The concept we can agree with. We want, frankly, as much of the money as we can get swapped over to Pillar 2, for obvious reasons. They want it kept in Pillar 1 for the reasons we understand.
Mr Manning: Maybe I can add one further thing to that. It is important to note that the proposal that the Commission has made for national envelopes is for a closed list, so there are only specific things that Member States can spend money on. As I said earlier on, we are not over-enthusiastic about any of them, but it could be worse; there could be much more distorting things in the national envelopes, which comes back to the earlier question about green harvesting. What we want to do most of all is to avoid measures coming into the national envelopes which try and perpetuate the lack of market focus that we see at the moment. So as far as we are concerned, we can probably live with the measures which are in the national envelopes; we would not be keen about adding to them. What we have said through the negotiation so far is that we can understand a lot of money going to the countries who have to make the biggest adaptations at the start of the transition period, but that, as you get more into a steady state, it would make much more sense in many ways to start reducing the amount of money which is being spent on the wine regime both in terms of saving money but, also, maybe, spending money more sensibly through RDR because I think there is a greater range of programmes that can be introduced to address Member States' concerns.

Q912 *Lord Plumb:* Interestingly, you said that you would welcome that money going to Pillar 2. Is there not a danger that Pillar 2 then would be used for other purposes? If the principle is established, then some countries may start using the money from Pillar

2 for growth and for some of the things that they are already doing.

Lord Rooker: It would give more flexibility but they would have to match the spending. There would be a difference in that respect. There is a principle issue here. The details are going to be very awkward and we are going to have to live with what is some uncomfortable detail. Splitting up the money based on former production and former subsidy—the amount of acreage under growth—obviously disadvantages the UK. The three large producers would receive over €200 million each and we would get about €180,000 to €200,000—it is that kind of scale. We are just not on the radar. There would be more flexibility in the Member States not to be doing crude subsidies. Also, they would have to pay more themselves. That is the thing that may stop them of course; the idea they would have to match funding. There would be pressure on the Member States not to do silly things.

Q913 *Lord Plumb:* My fear was that there might be too much flexibility and, therefore, it could be used for other purposes. We have seen it happen in the past in other areas. Anyway, I take your point. You say you support the Commission's proposals, and we are relieved to hear that you support the majority of our proposals so far. The Commissioner, Mrs. Fischer-Boel, has said that she sees this as budget neutral. Is it not your intention to try to cut the budget to use money for other purposes rather than continue the expenditure of €1.3 billion, which is the expenditure at the moment on the whole thing? What steps do you have in mind to achieve this? Might I say, my Lord Chairman, that in our meetings with a number of people in France, when we went down to Languedoc and to Bordeaux, I felt—and I am sure we felt as a group—that the majority of growers there are prepared to accept change. In fact, I heard a Frenchman say that he did not want subsidies. That is the first time in my 40 years of involvement that I have ever heard a Frenchman say he did not want subsidies! So they are prepared to accept change. Yet we met one Senator who said: "We will not accept any changes at all until Italy agrees that they planted, I think it was, 20,000 hectares illegally last year." If this goes on, it will go on for ever and a day. It is really the budget issue. How do you see this? Should there not be savings there if the Commission's proposals go through?

Lord Rooker: I think the answer to your question is yes, there should be savings but they are not going to be immediate. As part of the price, I think, for getting what is a fairly large cultural change, as well as economic and management change, we are starting off with this new regime, as it were, budget-neutral, is a way to try and win support. In other words, the arguments can be made that these things are not being done necessarily to save money. Obviously, it is our intention to move away completely from subsidies long term on all production in the EU, but to get the changes we have to pay a price. This is a substantial change. The budget is the maximum spend—there cannot be any increase on that. It would be nicc if one could say there would be substantial cuts now, but that would probably negate the negotiating position of trying to get the change in. The answer to your question is yes, we do want savings, and in the long term we would expect to get them.

Q914 *Chairman:* Will we have a chance of looking at that when the new financial perspective comes up?

Lord Rooker: Yes, but we need to get this change under our belt first.

Q915 *Lord Plumb:* I think, my Lord Chairman, certainly in the Languedoc region there was much talk of, say, the £5 bottle. When we get to the Bordeaux region, of course, they quite arrogantly say: "There is nobody who can compete with us for the quality wines we produce", and nobody argues with that. However, they realise they are up against it and, when we see the graph of the import now of New World wines, they know very well they are out of business before long if they do not accept change. That is a very strong argument we have got for bringing about that change for that type of wine, which is a popular wine—the sort of lunchtime or evening drinkable wine—which they have gone off in France, according to the figures, but it is being drunk elsewhere.

Chairman: We did come across quite a lot of entrepreneurial wine makers, but very conservative wine politicians.

Lord Rooker: There is inevitability, in some ways; you do find areas where the industry has seen the writing on the wall because they have seen their balance sheets. Sometimes the industry does lead the politicians. I can give you examples but I do not dare give them at the moment here—home-grown examples—which I am currently dealing with, where it is quite clear the industry is somewhat ahead of the politicians. So that is not unusual. Therefore, that is good because it is better if it is that way round. That way you can see a possibility of progress.

Q916 *Chairman:* Can we go on to promotion. When we were taking evidence, everybody was saying that support for marketing was very important. Then, when we asked and probed a little bit about what "marketing" meant, it turned into "promotion"; and then, when we asked what "promotion" meant, it meant advertising in non-EU countries. I do not think that is going to deliver much benefit. The crying need is to improve marketing in the proper and full sense of getting the producer closer to the consumer and those sorts of connections. What is your view on giving over a tenth of national envelope money to, basically, advertising in non-EU countries?

Lord Rooker: If they thought promotion was just advertising EU wines, let us say, in Third Countries, and they do, let us say, keep the labelling the same as they do now, it is not going to sell anything. It does not matter how much they advertise, if you put labels on bottles that people cannot understand, which is almost the exact opposite of what they have been doing in Australia and New Zealand and the others—South Africa and Chile: they have learnt their lesson. In other words, they have got to be consumer-orientated; so it cannot be just advertising EU wines in Third Countries. I think promotional money is probably quite useful; it could assist in some ways, probably, in some aspects of the way their own internal market is organised. The advertising is appalling in getting issues on the labelling and explaining what the wines are like, and doing the brands, as it were. I am afraid the variety of brands and labels, particularly in France (which are the wines I know better than the other two, I have to say) are enormously complicated. I do not think just advertising European wine is going to work; they have got to do a lot more than that to get across to the consumer. They have to realise that they are advertising to consumers and individual people—not industries. If they do not make that breakthrough, however much is spent on promotion, it is not going to work. If the money can be used also to help with the integration of companies and producers, and maybe put more vertical integration into their production methods, that would be of assistance. I would look on that as promotion. Promotion is not necessarily advertising.

Lord Plumb: €120 million of European money every year for promotion.

Q917 ***Lord Palmer:*** Minister, I would like to ask you about the ban on new plantings. Are you able to shed more light on the Commission's proposals? It looks as though, even after the ban on plantings is lifted, Member States will still be able to prohibit new plantings in areas which produce GI wines. In reality, is this simply not giving the whip hand to the producers in these areas, so that they can keep out new competition? How do you envisage you are going to play this?

Lord Rooker: That is where I invite Robin to expand on the details, but that is obviously an area of concern. The way that they have argued the ban on new plantings, it has been an economic fiddle, in some ways, of trying to manipulate the market, and it has not been very successful. From our point of view, this is an area where we are concerned because the English wine industry is growing. As you know from your researches, we are on the borderline of the 25,000 hectore-litre over the five year average, and we will certainly break that during the period of 2010–2013. With the ban on plantings extended to 2013, it causes difficulty and, therefore, we need an increase on that 25,000 hectore-litre, and we will seek to negotiate that. We may have to by supporting the Commission's 2013 figure in order to stop the other Member States extending to 2015 or 2016, which is what they intend to try and do, according to what has been said in the last few days. I think we need the market. If someone is going to plant a vineyard, they ought to do it in the knowledge that they think they can sell and market the product. That is the point. There should not be a ban on plantings. They take the risk of planting; it should not be for the individual producers to say: "Ah, we are going to ban so-and-so planting extra, because that protects our little empire". That is quite unacceptable—quite unacceptable. We want the issue to be consumer-orientated: farmers take the risk of planting; they know their market—or one has to assume they do but they obviously do not know much about the market because they have been so protected from it in many ways. We cannot possibly countenance a system of having bans on plantings, then trying to extend it and then individuals trying to decide who can plant what and where. That has got to be down to the individual producer. That is our view and that is the view we will take to the negotiations.

Mr Manning: It is very hard, coming from the UK, to understand why the producer Member States attach so much significance to the planting rights scheme and consider it a success, when you consider the problems facing the wine sector at the moment. The problems facing the wine sector are due to a complete disconnect between the production decisions in many circumstances and the wishes of consumers. We are only going to get that market focus as a consequence of, as we said earlier on, removing the market intervention measures, but also freeing up the industry to be able to react to market signals. We are quite concerned about the proposal for an extension to the planting ban when the English industry has been working on the basis that they can carry on planting and responding to market demand on the basis that the ban would end at the end of 2010.

Q918 ***Chairman:*** You seem to be saying that, although the Commission is proposing an extension, the real fight is going to be on preventing that extension going even further?

Lord Rooker: Absolutely, yes, which is why, as I said, in supporting the Commission, because we think they have been quite brave and bold, as their original plan in supporting that, we may have to have some give and take on other issues, because to keep to 2013 is pretty important, as far as we are concerned. According to the reports I have received they are going to be under enormous pressure from some of what I might call the old-fashioned producers to extend that date.

Chairman: Let us look at one of the other areas: enrichment.

Q919 ***Viscount Ullswater:*** Minister, you mentioned enrichment as being one of the particular aspects which you thought was a difficult one, especially for the Northern European wine producers—the use of sucrose has been commonplace. Enrichment through the use of must has been supported financially, and I notice, also, that it seems that—and I do not quite understand what it means—under Rural Development Member States will be able to provide investment support to wine producers who have to change their use of sugar for enrichment to the use of must, which seems to be a subsidy in another form—under a different heading. Can you tell us your view about enrichment? What do you feel the British position would be about it? And anything else?

Lord Rooker: I have to say that I know nothing about wine production—consumption yes, but not production! I have visited one English vineyard in Kent, a very modern, private sector, investment winery. I did not know about enrichment until I went there; I did not know about sugar. I suppose, as an ordinary layperson in this respect, I was a bit surprised until it was explained to me in terms of low sugars and higher acids in the northern part of Europe. It is not just an English issue, obviously; it is a particular issue in Germany. The fact of the matter is that it would be very costly on our industry—an increase in production costs of 10 to 20%. The northern Member States are the ones that currently use it, and, of course, we would have to import the must. Apparently, there is only one producer of that and it so happens it is in Germany.

Mr Manning: Traditionally, as we understand it, English producers have imported German must, where they have used must instead of sugar. But effectively, if the ban came in, then it would mean that, instead of being able to use sugar as the enrichment agent, which you do need in the north of the community because we get less sun, particularly in years like this, they would have to use grape juice, and the grape juice would be obtained from an existing producer Member State—like Spain or Portugal.

Lord Rooker: And it would lower the quality because they want to limit it, so it has an effect on the wine strength of 2%, whereas at the moment it is 3.5%. One of the reasons for this, allegedly, is to reduce production overall. We do not want to reduce production; our industry is growing. It is tiny—tiny—but, to their credit, they are winning gold medals in Paris and flourishing. With climate change it is one that will be expanding—it will never be massive. I do not know where we are on the negotiation, but the effect of this change, which will sharpen the negotiation, is disproportionate on northern European Member States. It is not going to affect the Spanish, the Portuguese, the Italians, probably the French—certainly not the southern French—so it is disproportionate if we do not negotiate our way out of this issue.

Q920 ***Viscount Ullswater:*** Do you think there is any chance of getting them to drop that particular issue?

Lord Rooker: I will leave Robin to answer that because he is hot from the "war front".

Viscount Ullswater: It does seem to be such a peculiarly inappropriate thing to be so firm on, when so many of the northern European states have been using sugar. Of all the people at the moment, it is going to be southern Italy and Sicily.

Q921 ***Chairman:*** Before Robin does answer, when we were over in Brussels we interviewed the German representative and he was very laid back and relaxed about it. His view was that it always comes in, it always starts off as something to do and it is knocked down—it is there to be knocked down.

Mr Manning: I think that would be our view as well. There is so much opposition to this. It is seen for what it is: it is just a crude mechanism to try and use extra grape juice, and it does not really take account of the fact that what we want is a wine industry which is market-oriented and responds to commercial opportunity. Just to answer your point on the RDR question, the first thing I would say is that we do not think that the ban on sugar will last the negotiation. That is our starting position. However, if it did, then the sorts of programmes which are being talked about would be introduced under Rural Development plans, and it would be for Member States to take a view on whether or not this is the sort of thing that they would want to invest in. But, given the small amount of money which is going into Rural Development, as we have already said, I would think it would probably not be high on the list of priorities for any Member States to decide to spend money on that when most of the issues that they are concerned about relate to maintaining the social and environmental fabric of wine growing in their countries. So we would be looking primarily, I think, at agri-environment rather than investment money of this nature. However, that is not to say that it would not happen; the whole purpose of RDR—and this is why it is match-funded—is that it is for Member States to take their own national decisions on things that they want to spend money on, albeit that they have to pass the Commission's test; they have to make sure that they are compatible with the regulation and that their plans are appropriate and are passed by the Commission.

Q922 ***Baroness Jones of Whitchurch:*** We have already touched a little bit on the issue of labelling and we received compelling evidence, I would say, from some of the New World producers who had designed the labels on the bottles to respond to what they felt the consumers wanted to know, and their market share is evidence of how successful that has been. Do you think that the Commission is missing a trick here, with its reformed wine classification still having the link between quality and geography? Are they missing a trick? Are we still being stuck in that old-fashioned route, which actually most consumers do not understand, and we are still mystifying the labelling far more than we should be doing? Is there an argument for saying that people should be able put whatever they like on the labels as long as it is truthful and honest—just those very basic things, which is what you would get on most packaging of food or drink?
Lord Rooker: I think you are right there. As I say, we are very supportive of the Commission's proposals. We are a bit disappointed in the way that they seem to imply embodying the existing geographical pre-requisites remaining on labels. If one takes the English consumer, as the one I know, we have had a phenomenal increase in the consumption of wine but no one is going to say people in this country are wine buffs—part of the cognorcent; of wine-drinking. They have embraced it as alternatives to beer, lager and spirits. However, what they want is clarity on the labels, as you say. If people go into a pub, they do not walk in and call for a glass of French wine by the location, and all that sort of thing; they will ask for a glass of Chardonnay or a glass of Sauvignon. They want it clear; they do not want the label cluttered up. In a way, one has only got to look at the contrast of the labels between New World and what has happened in France and, also, in Spain, to see the difference. I know we have got the brands of Champagne and Bordeaux, and all that, but that is slightly different to the thousands of others across Spain, Germany and France. So they have missed a trick, to an extent, and they have got to learn that this regime is not for the producer, it is for the consumer. If the consumers carry on as they are, when you look at the figures, Europe is the biggest importer of wine, the biggest consumer of wine and, at the moment still, the biggest exporter of wine, but it is on a downward path. We will carry on being a big consumer, I am sure of that. We would like to carry on being the biggest exporter, but we will lose that if we cannot export to countries because of the lack of clarity and simplicity. We think they all go and need an A level in how to understand wine, and that is nice, if you want to do that, but the average punter will not do that, and that is what they have got to get more into. Some more work needs to be done on that, I think, with the Commission; they need to be taken on one side and explained. I think they understand the facts of the situation—certainly looking at these documents—I do not think there is any doubt in the Commission. But they are trying to make a major change, so they are trying to bring these old-fashioned, conservative producers along with them. It is their culture, it is their heritage. One has to think of what happened and not say to people: "You're stupid; you've been wasting your time; you don't know what you're doing." You cannot use that kind of language to them; you have got to be a bit more sophisticated about it. But they have missed a trick, in some ways, by sticking to those prerequisites on the labels. We will try and correct them in the negotiations because they are only tinkering with the system at the moment—with what the proposal is, really.

Q923 ***Lord Palmer:*** I ought to declare an interest as the recipient of a Single Farm Payment.
Lord Rooker: You have got it then?

Q924 ***Chairman:*** He is Scottish!
Lord Rooker: Oh dear!

Q925 ***Lord Palmer:*** It is, however, proposed to bring vineyards and, indeed, grubbed-up vineyards within the ambit of the Single Farm Payment. Some could regard that as a step in the right direction in that it will bring the Wine CMO closer to the 2003 CAP reforms and perhaps encourage some wine-growers to diversify. Of course, not every wine-grower is able to diversify, as we are aware. But is it not also arguable that the Single Farm Payment is just another subsidy which will go to profitable as well as unprofitable wine producers?
Lord Rooker: That happens now with the Single Farm Payment. The one good thing about the Single Farm Payment, of course, is that it is decoupled from production. There is a big advantage in some ways in bringing all land that is producing food and drink into Single Farm Payments to get clarity within the system. As you implied in your question, anyone with a vineyard, if they grub it up, can use the land and get a new entitlement under Single Farm Payments. If there is an existing vineyard (and one takes the English situation that we are in now) which would not be in a Single Farm Payment (most of them are quite tiny), the only way they can get a new entitlement—because the entitlements are all fixed from 2005—is to grub-up the vineyard, and there is not much sign of anyone wanting to do that; it is the opposite way round. However, they can buy entitlements under the trading system of Single Farm Payments, and they can, of course, if you like, swap

the fields around, if they want to replant, because obviously all our farms are fairly mixed. The Single Farm Payment is there for the foreseeable future. It is not tied to production of the goods (to that extent it is a benefit) and, secondly, to obtain it you have got to conform with cross-compliance and the other rules. I understand about 50% of the vineyards probably do already comply across Europe. However, there is an overall benefit for it as far as we can see. It is not giving Single Farm Payments for existing vineyards, so it is not new in that sense. There is no new entitlement created; the entitlements are fixed, and the only way you can get a new entitlement is if you grubbed-up the vineyard and did not replant it somewhere else—but that is not likely to happen to us.

Mr Manning: If I can just clarify one point on that, as far as the grubbing-up scheme is concerned, it is subject to the same threshold as the planting ban, so in the UK the grubbing-up scheme would not apply because we are under 25,000 hectore-litre. However, Lord Rooker is absolutely right, in any other country the only new entitlements which are being created by the wine reform occur where the farmer is actually undergoing a fundamental change in land use and, effectively, going out of wine production.

Q926 ***Chairman:*** At some time in the relatively near future we may be asking you about the future of the Single Farm Payment, but we will leave that for the moment.

Lord Plumb: ***We look forward to that!***

Lord Rooker: I am quite happy to talk about Single Farm Payments; we have done very well this year compared to last year, but we still need to do a lot better and we expect to do better next year.

Chairman: I think we are just wondering how far into the future we will have Single Farm Payments. Never mind—do not go there now! A last question, appropriately, from Lord Moynihan.

Q927 ***Lord Moynihan:*** The way ahead. It would be very helpful indeed if you could give us an indication of the status of some of the negotiations. You might want to elaborate a little bit further on that and on how you see them coming to a conclusion on the timing and content. We are conscious of the fact that there was some opposition to the Commission's proposals at the Agriculture Council last week. I just wondered if you could give us some indicators as to how you see this all playing out.

Lord Rooker: Certainly you will get much more detail on that from Robin. Basically, we are very supportive. We want it completed as soon as possible. There will be no delay from our point of view, but obviously there may be rearguard actions from other Member States, as we have implied, I think, from what has been said this morning. Negotiations have started in the Wine and Spirits Working Group, and I think we have finished for July now and we will start again in September. I am in no position to say whether they would conclude in the current Presidency; the Portuguese want to make as much progress as possible and we want to give them every support, if it can be concluded. As I say, from our point of view, we do not want any delay. Obviously, it goes with the seasons as well, from that point of view. I do not know quite when it would kick in once it is agreed because then you have got the growing seasons—but as soon as possible.

Q928 ***Lord Plumb:*** Will it be settled before the sugar regime?

Lord Rooker: No, I am not going into sugar. I think that would be highly dangerous of me, at the moment.

Mr Manning: I can expand on wine—not on sugar, unfortunately. We have really just started the process. We have had six days of working groups in two-and-a-half weeks, so we feel quite shattered, actually, because it is really hard going. We are only about 50% of the way through the first reading of the document and, while we have touched on some controversial issues, such as the planting ban and the grubbing-up scheme, we have not even considered things such as wine-making practices or enrichment, which I think will be equally difficult. The Presidency have tabled another five days of working groups through September, and I think the aim then will be to have completed the first reading and for the Commission to take a view on the comments which have been received and decide where they think they can move on certain areas, where they feel that the points which Member States are making are right and there is the clarification necessary. There will be a further level of technical discussion but, ultimately, where we have a dossier as difficult and as important as this, it will be settled at a political level. Whether that is possible in December in the final Portuguese Council, I do not know; that will be the aim—to try and get political agreement then. Whether that is possible, as I say, there is a lot of divergence of opinion between, let us say, producers and non-producers, in terms of the way forward, over really fundamental issues, such as what you can put on a label and what you cannot put on a label. Should producers be allowed to take an economic decision and grub-up their vines? Or do they have to stay in production even though they are not going to be economic? Should we constrain the industry from growing and responding to market opportunity? Or should we just allow uneconomic producers to stay in production and go bankrupt because they no longer receive market support? How will we define the GIs and the PDOs, the new system of authorisation of varieties? So there is a lot of work to do. It is a very challenging dossier but, actually, very interesting as well. We have submitted an Explanatory Memorandum where we have tried to bring out some of the issues as well for your consideration.

Chairman: When we all set out on this we did not know a great deal about it. As the Minister said, we are more interested in the consumption side than the production side. The more all of us have got into it, however, it is an absolutely fascinating area and crying out for reform.

Q929 ***Viscount Ullswater:*** One further point: is the *de minimis* rule being negotiated at all—the 25,000 hectore-litre? Is it being considered to move that up a tiny bit? It might help the UK industry.

Lord Rooker: Obviously, I have not been party to the negotiations. Certainly from our point of view we want that raised.

Q930 ***Viscount Ullswater:*** Is that part of the negotiations, strictly speaking?

Mr Manning: The whole of that is to be negotiated, and the 25,000 hectore-litre appears in two articles of the regulations. On both sides we are saying that we want that up substantially—at least double—as part and parcel of our agreement to allow the planting ban to be extended to 2013. We could not really have one without the other.

Q931 ***Chairman:*** I do not know if you wish to say anything in conclusion?

Lord Rooker: Thank you.

Chairman: Thank you. Three-quarters of an hour!

Printed in the United Kingdom by The Stationery Office Limited
10/2007 380290 19585

ISBN 978-0-10-401157-7

9 780104 011577